the BROADWAY junior

COLLECTION

_____
Name

_____
Character

Annie jr.

Special thanks to John Higgins, Jim Luigs, Steve Zawel, Cindy Ripley and the students at the Enrico Fermi School for the Performing Arts in Yonkers, NY and Gowanda Elementary School in Gowanda, NY.

MTi ™
MUSIC THEATRE INTERNATIONAL

EXCLUSIVELY DISTRIBUTED BY

HAL•LEONARD®

TABLE OF CONTENTS

Introduction

Libretto

Vocal

To the Actor

You are about to begin **rehearsals** for a production of *Annie,* one of the most popular Broadway musicals ever created. "Rehearsing" refers to the process of learning and practicing a **dramatic work** (such as a play or musical) in order to perform it for an audience. It involves a great deal of time, hard work and commitment, and is far from easy. Because a musical uses spoken words, songs and dances to tell a story, you may be called upon to act, sing *and* dance in your production — that's a lot to rehearse! But there's nothing more exciting than opening night, when all that effort pays off in front of a cheering audience.

The process begins with this book, which is virtually identical to the ones professional actors use to rehearse. It will be your most important resource as you prepare for your production, and you should always bring it to rehearsals, even after you have memorized your part. You never know when you might forget a line and need to look it up!

The main section of the book contains the **dialogue, lyrics** and **stage directions** for the musical.

- Dialogue refers to the words the characters speak in the show. The complete dialogue of a show is called the **book** of the show; therefore, the "book" you hold in your hands contains the "book" of the show.

- Lyrics are the words the characters sing in the show.

- Stage directions describe how the show will look to your audience, including the physical appearance of the stage, the location and position of each character **onstage**, and any important physical actions performed by the characters. Sometimes stage directions also help the actors and **director** (the person responsible for guiding the entire production) understand why characters say and do certain things. The reason behind a character's actions is called his or her **motivation**.

Together, dialogue, lyrics and stage directions make up the **libretto** (or **script**) of the show. The script is usually divided into two main sections called **acts,** which are in turn divided into **scenes,** each scene usually taking place in a different location (or **setting**). In performance, acts are often separated by a brief ten- to fifteen-minute **intermission,** during which members of the audience can get up, stretch their legs, visit the restroom and otherwise refresh themselves. Your production of *Annie* will consist of only one act, so your performance won't include an intermission.

The following diagram shows a page from the libretto, and how each of the show's elements is represented in the script.

Block letters indicate the beginning of a scene.

The current scene number appears centered at the top of each page.

Stage directions are in italics and indented.

The page number appears at the top corner of each page.

Scene 3   *Page 49*

SCENE THREE

(The LIGHTS come up as MISS HANNIGAN goes into her office, which contains a desk, a rocking chair, and a rolling office chair. On the desk is a cathedral-style radio.[46] TESSIE runs in from STAGE LEFT and goes up to MISS HANNIGAN)

A black bar indicates the beginning of a song or **musical number.** White letters indicate the title of the musical number and the character or characters who will sing it.

#10   Little Girls   (Miss Hannigan)

TESSIE

Miss Hannigan, you know your souvenir pillow from Coney Island?[47]

MISS HANNIGAN

Yeah.

TESSIE

Molly just threw up on it.

(MISS HANNIGAN threatens TESSIE. TESSIE runs off STAGE LEFT; MISS HANNIGAN sits in the office chair. SHE gets up, holding a broken doll on which she has just sat)

Dialogue appears in regular type.

MISS HANNIGAN
LITTLE GIRLS,
LITTLE GIRLS...
EVERYWHERE I TURN,
I CAN SEE THEM.
LITTLE GIRLS,
LITTLE GIRLS...
NIGHT AND DAY
I EAT, SLEEP AND BREATHE THEM.

SOME WOMEN ARE DRIPPING WITH DIAMONDS,
SOME WOMEN ARE DRIPPING WITH PEARLS.
LUCKY ME!
LUCKY ME!
LOOK AT WHAT I'M DRIPPING WITH:
LITTLE GIRLS!

Lyrics are in capital letters and are indented

Character names in boldface indicate which character speaks the next line of dialogue or sings the next lyric.

The section in the back of the book contains the printed music for all of the songs (or **musical numbers**) in *Annie.* The complete music and lyrics of a show make up the show's score. This section is called the **vocal book** because it includes only the parts of the score that are to be sung.

Because your rehearsal book contains both the show's libretto and vocal book, it is called the **libretto/vocal book.**

How to start talking like a bigshot actor

As you read and rehearse *Annie,* you will no doubt encounter some unfamiliar theatrical terms. People who work in the theatre have coined many words and phrases that make it easier for them to talk about what and where things happen on a stage or in a theatre. You should try to learn and use these terms, as rehearsing is much easier when everyone speaks the same language.

The term **"theatre"** (sometimes spelled "theater") can be used in many different ways. It may refer to a play or musical, a performance of a play or musical, the quality of such a performance, a building in which plays and musicals are presented, a room in which plays and musicals are presented, or the community of people who work to create and perform plays or musicals. This means you can go to a "theatre" to see a piece of "theatre" which is very good "theatre" and which represents the best "theatre" has to offer!

"Curtain" is another word with multiple uses. Usually, it refers to the heavy curtain that can be lowered across the front of the stage to hide the stage from the audience. It may also refer to the beginning of a show (or act), when the heavy curtain is raised to reveal the stage. It may also refer to the end of a show (or act), when the heavy curtain is dropped!

The **stage** is, of course, the area from which actors perform for an audience. The **house** is the area where the audience sits to watch the performance. Anything on the stage and within view of the audience is said to be **onstage**; anything outside the view of the audience is said to be **offstage.** The entire area offstage is the **backstage** area. "Stage" can also be used to describe the action of planning out how something will be carried out onstage: a director "stages a scene" by planning out where and how the actors will move and interact onstage during a particular section of the play or musical.

The various onstage, offstage and backstage areas vary from theatre to theatre. Some theatres have an **apron,** a section of the stage that extends forward in front of the main curtain. Some theatres have a sunken area in front of the stage called the **orchestra pit,** from which any musicians involved in the production perform.

Most theatres have **wings,** which are areas to the side of the stage, just out of the audience's view. Actors who are about to come onstage are often said to be "waiting in the wings." Also hidden from the audience is the area above the stage, called the **fly** or **fly space.** Sometimes long black curtains called **legs** hang from above the stage and at its sides, to further hide the wings and fly space.

Just beyond the backstage area are the **dressing rooms,** where the actors change into and out of their costumes before, after and during the performance. Most theatres also have a **green room** closeby, where actors can rest while waiting for their scenes.

The areas of the house also vary from theatre to theatre. Most theatres have a house consisting of one level, called the **orchestra section** (because it sits on the same level as the orchestra pit). Larger theatres may have a house with two or more levels (or **tiers**). The second tier is usually called the **mezzanine,** the third the **balcony.**

In addition to learning the names of the different areas in a theatre, you should familiarize yourself with the various theatrical equipment that will surround you onstage and offstage. **Backdrops** are large pieces of painted paper, cloth or other material which hang behind acting areas to represent different locations. They usually hang from metal pipes suspended overhead called **battens. Cycloramas** or **cycs** (pronounced "sykes") are special backdrops that hang at the back of the stage and are often lit to represent the sky. Sometimes backdrops and cycloramas are supplemented with **flats,** wooden frames with material stretched across them. These, too, are painted to represent different settings. The entire physical environment onstage in any given scene is known as a **set,** and may include backdrops, flats, furniture and **props** (onstage objects used by the actors during the show).

The set is usually lit by **floodlights** and other types of theatrical lighting equipment, which hang from the battens and from the sides of the house. These lights are controlled by a **master lighting board** at the back of the theatre. Most theatre lights are fixed on one area of the stage and never move or change their focus. **Spotlights** or **follow spots**, on the other hand, can be used to follow a person who is moving around onstage. These powerful lights are usually located at (and operated from) the back of the house.

Microphones may also hang from the battens, to amplify the sound of the actors' voices. Special types of microphones that may be used include **foot mics** (flat microphones which are arranged along the front edge of the stage) and **body** or **lavolier mics** (portable microphones strapped to the actors' bodies). Like the lights, the microphones are controlled from the back of the theatre by a **sound board** or **mixing board** (so-called because it is used to "mix" the sounds from the various microphones onstage into one sound, which is then played through amplifiers in the house). Sometimes onstage actors want to hear the "mixed" sound the audience is hearing, so they can adjust their volume onstage accordingly. An amplifier placed onstage to allow actors to hear what the audience hears is called a **monitor.** Sometimes monitors are also placed in the dressing rooms and in the green room, so actors backstage can keep track of what is happening onstage.

The most important terms you must learn are the ones theatre professionals use to describe the position of people and things onstage. Each section of the stage has a specific name. When you stand at the center of the stage and face the audience:

- **upstage** is the area behind you;
- **downstage** is the area in front of you;
- **stage right** is the area to your right;
- **stage left** is the area to your left; and
- **centerstage** is the area where you are standing.

These terms can be combined; for example, the area to your right and behind you is **upstage right** (sometimes shortened to **up right**). They stay the same no matter what direction you face or where you are located onstage or in the theatre; for example, the section of the stage farthest away from the audience and to its left is always **upstage right**.

The terms are also used to describe the relative position of people and things onstage; for example, in the following diagram, if you are at point A, you are **upstage center**. A table located at point B is at **centerstage right,** but is said to be **downstage right** of you.

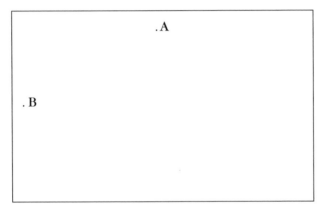

Audience

Another useful set of terms describes what happens onstage during the show:

- an actor **enters** or makes an **entrance** when that actor steps onstage;
- an actor **exits** or makes an **exit** when that actor leaves the stage;
- an actor **crosses** when that actor moves from one place onstage to another;
- an actor **counters** when that actor moves to fill the space left by an actor who has just **crossed;** and
- a **cue** is any line or action that triggers another line or action.

Last (but not least), there are terms given to the various people with whom you will work. The actors in a show are collectively known as the **cast.** ("Cast" can also be used to refer to the process of choosing a cast for a show.) The people who work backstage during a show are known as the **crew.** Together, the cast and the crew are known as the **company.** The company is headed by the **creative team,** which consists of the people "in charge": the **producer** (who makes sure everyone does his or her job), the **designers** (who design and/or create the sets, costumes, sound system and lighting), the **technical director** (who coordinates the construction and painting of the sets, the hanging of the lights and the set-up of the sound system), the director, the **music director** (who is in charge of teaching the music and maintaining its quality) and the **choreographer** (who creates and teaches the dances). You will also have a **stage manager** who is responsible for making sure rehearsals and performances run smoothly and on schedule.

There are three very important members of the creative team whom you will never see at rehearsals: the writers of the musical. Although their contribution to the show was completed long ago, you will be working with them by bringing their words and music to life onstage. These writers include the **composer** (who wrote the music), the **lyricist** (who wrote the lyrics) and the **librettist** or **bookwriter** (who wrote the book). (You will notice the word "libretto" can refer to the book of a show, as well as to the book *and* lyrics of a show. This can be confusing. . .again, no one said acting was easy!)

How to destroy your script like a professional

Most professional actors feel libretto/vocal books are worthless until marked up, underlined and run-through with a highlighting pen. The reason for this will become clear as you begin rehearsals.

As you rehearse, you will find although your libretto/vocal book provides you with lines, music, lyrics and basic stage directions, it leaves countless details to the imagination of you and your director. This is part of the excitement of live theatre: unlike film and television (where performances, sets, costumes and camera shots are forever frozen in place), a piece of live theatre changes with each production and performance. The same words and music may be interpreted in countless different ways, making each production and performance unique. It is up to your director to make the final decisions as to which interpretation is right for your production. To this end, your director will give you instructions (or **notes**) on your **blocking** (where, when and how you move onstage), **stage business** (the actions you perform onstage) and **line readings** (how you interpret your lines and lyrics). Your director will also help you understand your character (or **role**), why your character does certain things (your character's motivation), how your character interacts with other characters, and the significance of your character to the entire musical. Meanwhile, your music director and choreographer will teach you your character's songs and dances (the dances in a show are known as the show's **choreography**) and give notes on how to perform them.

You will be responsible for remembering *all* of these notes and carrying them out in rehearsal and performance!

The best way to do this is to copy any notes you are given into the margins of your libretto/vocal book. In marking up your libretto/vocal book, you are "completing" the script of the show as it is interpreted by your director, music director and choreographer, and creating a guide to which you can refer if you should forget what to do during rehearsals. So don't feel bashful about writing in your book — that's what it's there for.

The following are suggestions on how to mark up your libretto/vocal book. Any system you use is fine, as long as you remember how to interpret your markings.

1. **Always** write your name legibly, either on the cover of your libretto/vocal book or in the space provided on the title page. Libretto/vocal books have a nasty way of getting lost or changing hands during rehearsals!

2. Mark your lines and lyrics with a brightly colored highlighting pen, to make your part stand out visually on the page. This will allow you to look up from your script during rehearsals, since it will be easier to find your place when you look back down.

MISS HANNIGAN

Yeah.

TESSIE

Molly just threw up on it.

> (*MISS HANNIGAN threatens TESSIE. TESSIE runs off STAGE LEFT; MISS HANNIGAN sits in the office chair. SHE gets up, holding a broken doll on which she has just sat*)

MISS HANNIGAN

LITTLE GIRLS,
LITTLE GIRLS...
EVERYWHERE I TURN,
I CAN SEE THEM.
LITTLE GIRLS,
LITTLE GIRLS...

---

3. Highlight or underline important stage directions, lines, lyrics and individual words; e.g., if your lyric reads "Everywhere I turn, I can see them" and your director wants you to stress the word "everywhere", highlight or underline that word in your libretto/vocal book.

MISS HANNIGAN

Yeah.

TESSIE

Molly just threw up on it.

(MISS HANNIGAN threatens TESSIE. TESSIE runs off STAGE LEFT; MISS HANNIGAN sits in the office chair. SHE gets up, holding a broken doll on which she has just sat)

MISS HANNIGAN

LITTLE GIRLS,
LITTLE GIRLS...
EVERYWHERE I TURN,
I CAN SEE THEM.
LITTLE GIRLS,
LITTLE GIRLS...

---

4. Save time and space by using the following standard abbreviations whenever possible:

ON: onstage	**CSL:** centerstage left
OFF: offstage	**USC:** upstage center
CS: centerstage	**USR:** upstage right
SR: stage right	**USL:** upstage left
SL: stage left	**DSC:** downstage center
US: upstage	**DSR:** downstage right
DS: downstage	**DSL:** downstage left
CSR: centerstage right	**X:** cross

You may use these abbreviations to modify other instructions (e.g., you could write "R hand up" to remind yourself to raise your right hand). You may also combine them in various ways (e.g., you could write "X DSR" to remind yourself to cross downstage right).

MISS HANNIGAN

Yeah.

TESSIE

Molly just threw up on it.

(MISS HANNIGAN threatens TESSIE. TESSIE runs off STAGE LEFT; MISS HANNIGAN sits in the office chair. SHE gets up, holding a broken doll on which she has just sat)

XDSR   **MISS HANNIGAN**

LITTLE GIRLS,
LITTLE GIRLS...
EVERYWHERE I TURN,
I CAN SEE THEM.
LITTLE GIRLS,
LITTLE GIRLS...

---

5. Draw diagrams to help clarify your blocking. For example, if you are instructed to walk in a circle around a table, you might draw a box to represent the table, then draw a circle around it with an arrowhead indicating the direction in which you're supposed to walk.

MISS HANNIGAN

Yeah.

TESSIE

Molly just threw up on it.

(MISS HANNIGAN threatens TESSIE. TESSIE runs off STAGE LEFT; MISS HANNIGAN sits in the office chair. SHE gets up, holding a broken doll on which she has just sat)

XDSR   **MISS HANNIGAN**

LITTLE GIRLS,
LITTLE GIRLS...
EVERYWHERE I TURN,
I CAN SEE THEM.
LITTLE GIRLS,
LITTLE GIRLS...

---

6. Mark your music with large commas, to remind yourself where to take breaths while singing.

7. Draw tiny pairs of glasses in your libretto or vocal book to indicate moments at which you need to pay special attention.

8. Draw stick figures to help you remember your choreography.

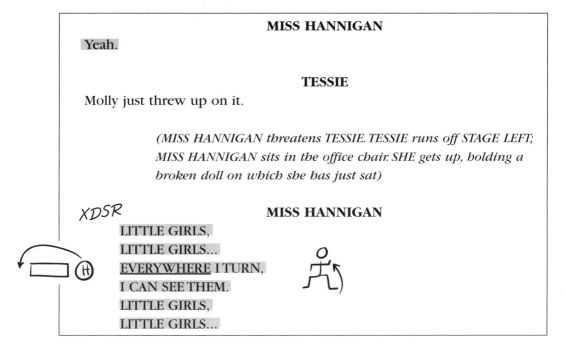

9. Although you should feel free to mark up your libretto/vocal book, be careful your script doesn't become so cluttered with notes you have a hard time finding your lines on the page! Don't get carried away with writing long, detailed notes or drawing elaborate pictures and diagrams. In most cases, a word or phrase will help you remember your notes. For example, if your director wants you to deliver a speech more deliberately, write the word "slower" next to the speech in the libretto. If the director complains of not being able to hear one of your lines, write "louder" or "volume" next to the line. If the director complains of not being able to understand what you are saying or singing, write "diction" next to the appropriate word or phrase to indicate you must improve your **diction** (the clarity and distinctness of each word you speak or sing).

Every good director, music director and choreographer likes actors to ask questions and come up with ideas of their own, so don't hesitate to write down any thoughts, questions and suggestions you might have regarding your blocking, stage business, line readings, motivation, musical interpretation and choreography. Remember, however, that although you may be encouraged to make your character "your own," the final decisions about your performance will always be made by the director.

What to expect in rehearsals . . .

It is important to know a little about the rehearsal process, so you can plan ahead and make the most of your time. Although your exact rehearsal schedule will be determined by your director, music director and choreographer, there is a general rehearsal plan which is followed by almost every production:

1. At the first rehearsal, the cast sits together and reads the script aloud.

2. The cast learns the music, blocking and choreography to the show, usually in that order.

3. The cast rehearses the book, songs and dances separately. Each song and dance is rehearsed separately, as is each scene in the book.

4. The cast rehearses each scene complete with all its components (book, songs and dances).

5. The cast rehearses the show in its entirety. A rehearsal in which you rehearse the entire show is called a **run-through.**

6. The cast moves its rehearsals into the theatre, if they have not already done so (earlier rehearsals are often held in smaller rehearsal rooms).

7. The cast members try on their costumes for the director and costume designer's approval. This is known as a **costume parade.**

8. The cast rehearses "in costume." These rehearsals are known as **dress rehearsals.**

9. The cast rehearses with the lights, sets and sound equipment (including microphones, if they are to be used). These rehearsals are known as **technical rehearsals** or "techs."

10. The director stages the **curtain call** at the final dress rehearsals. The curtain call is the last moment of the evening (after the show is over), when the cast members return onstage to take their bows.

The structure of each rehearsal will be the same. You will learn or practice the scene, song or dance indicated on the rehearsal schedule. Your director, music director or choreographer will then give you notes on your performance, and you will practice the scene, song or dance once more, keeping those notes in mind. Your early rehearsals will be **on-book** (i.e., you will rehearse with your libretto/vocal books in hand). Over the ensuing weeks and months, you will begin to memorize your lines, music, lyrics, choreography and blocking. You will eventually rehearse off-book (without your libretto/vocal books in hand). The sooner you get **off-book,** the better; it's much easier to act when you don't have to carry your script! Don't be afraid to start rehearsing from memory as soon as you feel you are ready — your stage manager will always have a libretto/vocal book open in order to remind you of your lines and blocking if you should forget them (this is known as **prompting**). If you forget a line, simply call, "Line!"

When you begin to rehearse in your performance space, be aware the theatre can be a dangerous place, especially when the technical elements (lights, sets and props) are in place. The typical stage is filled with heavy equipment, ropes, wires and potentially hazardous electronic equipment, and is not a place for horseplay or goofing off. It is also not a place for food and drink. Since working on a show can be very tiring, make sure you eat well (offstage, please!) and get enough sleep, not only so you have enough energy to rehearse and perform, but also so you can be alert to the potential dangers around you. If you are not feeling well at rehearsal, tell your director, music director or choreographer. Chances are they will let you sit out, go home or simply rehearse with less energy than usual, so you will not tire yourself out (this last solution is known as **marking**).

Being a member of the company of a show carries with it an enormous amount of responsibility. You are responsible not only to yourself, but also to your creative team and other company members. Every member of the cast and crew is vital to the success of the show. All actors — regardless of whether they play smaller roles or major (or **lead**) roles — rely on their fellow actors to speak each line and perform each stage action as rehearsed, and on the members of the crew to change the set, provide the necessary props and otherwise help out backstage. Likewise, each member of the crew relies on the actors; after all, without actors, there would be no performance! Because your actions affect those of the entire company, it is vital that you show up at each **call time** (the time at which you are expected at rehearsals or at the theatre before a performance), that you be punctual, and that you concentrate and follow instructions at all times. Use the chart and calendar on pages 15 - 19 to keep track of the scenes in which you are involved, the rehearsals for which you are scheduled and the call times for those rehearsals.

A final word...

The preceding pages contain a great deal of information, and you may feel a bit overwhelmed at how complicated it all seems. Don't worry, though — you'll be amazed how quickly you pick it all up once you start rehearsing. And the most important thing is to have fun. So get out there and "break a leg!" *

*Alarmingly violent theatre slang for "good luck"!

Scene/Character Breakdown

Use the following chart to keep track of the sections of the show in which your character is involved. If your character is involved in the scene or song indicated, write an "X" or make a check mark in the column labeled "Involved". If your character is not involved, write an "X" or make a check mark in the column labeled "Not involved". (You might find it useful to refer to the *Songs By Character* list on page 22 – 23.)

Your director will probably schedule rehearsals by scene number and song title; once you complete this chart, you can consult it to determine immediately whether you will be required at a particular rehearsal.

Your character: _____

Scene Number	Song	Involved	Not Involved
1			
	#3 Maybe		
	#5 Hard-Knock Life		
	#6 Hard-Knock Life — Reprise		
2			
	#8 Tomorrow		
3			
	#10 Little Girls		
	#11 Little Girls — Reprise		
4			
	#13 I Think I'm Gonna Like It Here		
5			
	#14 N.Y.C.		
6			
	#15 Easy Street		
7			
	#17 You Won't Be An Orphan For Long		
8			
	#18 Maybe — Reprise		
9			
	#19 You're Never Fully Dressed Without A Smile		
	#20 Easy Street — Reprise		
10			
	#21 I Don't Need Anything But You		
11			
	#22 Maybe — Second Reprise		
	#23 Tomorrow — Reprise		

Rehearsal Calendar

Write down the dates and times of your rehearsals in the spaces provided on the
following rehearsal calendar, along with the name of each scene and song to be
rehearsed.

For example:

Sunday	Monday	Tuesday	Wednesday	Thursday	Friday	Saturday
	1 2:30 pm: Scene 1	2 2:30 pm: Scene 2	3 2:30 pm: "Maybe"	4 3:00 pm: "Tomorrow"	5 OFF	6 OFF

Month: _____

Sunday	Monday	Tuesday	Wednesday	Thursday	Friday	Saturday

Month: _____

Sunday	Monday	Tuesday	Wednesday	Thursday	Friday	Saturday

Month: _____

Sunday	Monday	Tuesday	Wednesday	Thursday	Friday	Saturday

Month: _____

Sunday	Monday	Tuesday	Wednesday	Thursday	Friday	Saturday

Songs By Character

Characters

ANNIE

THE ORPHANS:

      MOLLY

      PEPPER

      DUFFY

      KATE

      TESSIE

      JULY

MISS HANNIGAN

BUNDLES McCLOSKEY

APPLE SELLER

DOGCATCHER

SANDY

LT. WARD

GRACE FARRELL

DRAKE

CECILLE

ANNETTE

MRS. GREER

MRS. PUGH

OLIVER WARBUCKS

STAR-TO-BE

MAN IN BROWNSTONE WINDOW

USHERETTE

RADIO ANNOUNCER

ROOSTER HANNIGAN

LILY ST. REGIS

SOUND EFFECTS MAN

BERT HEALY

PRESIDENT FRANKLIN DELANO ROOSEVELT

LOUIS HOWE

POLICEMAN

ADDITIONAL ORPHANS

SERVANTS

Notes on the Setting of ANNIE

On Orphanages

Orphanages in major cities were often cold, crowded places.

The first scene of *Annie* is set in an orphanage in New York City in 1933. An orphanage is an institution for the care of orphans.

In the 1800s, orphaned children were kept in "almshouses" with adults who were diseased, mentally ill and often abusive of the children. In some states, this practice continued as late as 1910. Children were "indentured," meaning they would earn their keep working for a tradesman, learning that tradesman's craft and developing skills they would use later in life. Often more emphasis was placed on the amount of work they could do rather than the care provided for them. By 1933, children were no longer kept with adults, but the emphasis was still on their labor. Life in these orphanages was often deplorable. These conditions slowly changed as professionally trained and licensed caretakers took over from the unskilled caretakers of the past. The 1930s saw a shift in thinking: people no longer felt work was good for children, and decided homes should be emphasized over institutions. There were the beginnings of what is now called the foster care system, in which the state pays foster parents to board orphaned children on a temporary basis until the children can be formally adopted.

On the Depression

The Great Depression was not only an economic crisis, it was an emotional blow which shattered the hopes and dreams of many Americans.

In 1933, the United States was in the depths of the Great Depression, the longest and worst economic crisis in American history. The stock market crash of 1929 had plunged the country into a period of deep financial and psychological distress, during which more than 10,000 banks and 90,000 businesses failed. Stocks lost about 80 percent of their value, farm prices fell by more than 50 percent and the gross national product declined at a rate of more than 10 percent per year. In 1933, almost one out of every four workers was unemployed. Ramshackle shanty-towns sprang up all over the nation to house the huge numbers of homeless Americans. People waited, often by the hundreds, in bread lines and soup lines in every American city hoping for a bit of food. Hope was at an all-time low as President Franklin Delano Roosevelt took office in March, 1933.

Libretto

| #1 | *Overture¹ (Optional)* | *(Orchestra)* |

SCENE ONE

| #2 | *Maybe — Underscore* | *(Annie)* |

(The CURTAIN rises on the New York City Municipal Orphanage — Girls' Annex.² "Maybe" underscores³ the following scene.

Shortly after three a.m. on a chilly morning in early December, 1933.

The stage is nearly dark. Asleep in the dormitory⁴ are [six] ORPHANS — MOLLY, the littlest, who is 6; KATE, the next-to-littlest, who is 7; TESSIE, the cry baby, who is 10; PEPPER, the toughest, who is 12; JULY, the quietest, who is 13; and DUFFY, the biggest, who is also 13.

NOTE: In addition to the six speaking ORPHANS, producers may wish to add ADDITIONAL ORPHANS. If so, dialogue written for the six speaking ORPHANS may be distributed, as necessary, among the ADDITIONAL ORPHANS — or the ADDITIONAL ORPHANS may simply be organized as GROUP ONE, GROUP TWO, GROUP THREE, etc.)

MOLLY
(Awaking from a dream and crying out)
Mama! Mama! Mommy!

PEPPER
Shut up!

DUFFY
Can't anybody get any sleep around here?

---

¹ **overture:** a piece of music played before the start of an opera or musical, often incorporating music from the work

² **municipal:** of or pertaining to a local government; **annex:** a subsidiary building or wing to a building

³ **underscore:** to play underneath a scene in order to clarify or heighten its mood

⁴ **dormitory:** a room for sleeping

MOLLY

Mama. Mommy.

PEPPER

I said shut your trap,[5] Molly.
> *(Shoves MOLLY to the floor,[6] DOWNSTAGE CENTER)*

JULY

Ahh, stop shovin' the poor kid. She ain't doin' nuthin' to you.[7]

PEPPER

She's keepin' me awake, ain't she?

JULY

No, you're keeping us awake —

PEPPER

You wanna make somethin' out of it?

JULY

How 'bout I make a pancake outta you?

> *(PEPPER and JULY fight)*

TESSIE

Oh my goodness, oh my goodness,[8] they're fightin' and I won't get no sleep all night. Oh my goodness, oh my goodness.

---

[5] **trap:** slang for "mouth"

[6] **Actor's note:** MOLLY should merely *appear* to get shoved to the floor. Remember, theatre is about illusion, not physical violence! Here's what to do: PEPPER should grab MOLLY'S shoulder and pull up (gently) while MOLLY flings herself to the floor. MOLLY should always be in control of the situation!

[7] Sometimes pages from a script will contain misspelled words (like "nuthin'" instead of "nothing"). These words should be pronounced as spelled, and are meant to reflect the characters' styles of speech.

[8] **Actor's note:** This exclamation ("oh my goodness, oh my goodness") is one of TESSIE'S **idiosyncrasies**. An **idiosyncrasy** is an unusual characteristic that makes someone special or memorable. See if you can discover or invent idiosyncrasies for the other characters in *Annie*.

(ANNIE, who is 11, runs in with a bucket. SHE has been up cleaning)

ANNIE

Pipe down,[9] all of ya. Go back to sleep.
(To MOLLY)
It's all right, Molly. Annie's here.

MOLLY

It was my Mama, Annie. We was ridin' on the ferryboat.[10] And she was holdin' me up to see all the big ships. And then I couldn't find her no more.

(ANNIE holds a hanky[11] for MOLLY)

ANNIE

Blow. It was only a dream, honey. Now, you gotta go back to sleep. It's after three o'clock.

MOLLY

Annie... read me your note.

ANNIE

Again?

MOLLY

Please?

ANNIE

Sure, Molly.

PEPPER

Here it comes again.

---

[9] **pipe down:** slang for "be quiet"

[10] **ferryboat:** a boat that brings passengers or goods across a narrow body of water such as a river. The Staten Island Ferry, for example, takes passengers from Manhattan to Staten Island, across New York Harbor.

[11] **hanky:** slang for "handkerchief"

ANNIE
(Takes a crumpled note[12] from her pocket, unfolds it and reads it to MOLLY[13])

"Please take good care of our little darling. Her name is Annie."

KATE
(Mockingly; she has heard this note read a thousand times before)

"She was born on October 28th. We will be back to get her soon."

PEPPER
(Mockingly)

"We have left half of a silver locket[14] around her neck and kept the other half —

PEPPER, DUFFY, KATE
— so that when we come back for her you will know that she's our baby."

TESSIE
Oh my goodness, oh my goodness, now they're laughing.

ANNIE
(To the OTHERS)

All right. Do you wanna sleep with your teeth insida your mouth or out!
(Lovingly folds her note and puts it back in her pocket)

MOLLY
Gee, I dream about havin' a mother and father again. But you're lucky. You really got 'em.

#3	*Maybe*	*(Annie)*

(See p. 108 for music)

ANNIE
(Fingering her locket)

I know.

---

[12] The note is crumpled because it is old; ANNIE has had it her entire life and has read it countless times. **Actor's note:** ANNIE should handle the note with great care; keep in mind it is her only link to her parents.

[13] **Actor's note:** ANNIE might be tempted to write her line on the note, so she won't have to memorize it; however, what if the ink gets smudged, or part of the note gets torn off? The safest thing is to memorize the line and pretend to read it off of the note.

[14] **locket:** a little case which usually hangs on a chain and is worn as either a necklace or bracelet

(ANNIE and MOLLY cuddle together on the floor)

Somewhere.

> MAYBE FAR AWAY
> OR MAYBE REAL NEARBY,
> HE MAY BE POURIN' HER COFFEE,
> SHE MAY BE STRAIGHT'NIN' HIS TIE!
>
> MAYBE IN A HOUSE
> ALL HIDDEN BY A HILL,

MOLLY

SHE'S SITTIN' PLAYIN' PIANO,

TESSIE

HE'S SITTIN' PAYIN' A BILL!

ANNIE

BETCHA THEY'RE YOUNG.
BETCHA THEY'RE SMART.

JULY

BET THEY COLLECT THINGS

DUFFY

LIKE ASHTRAYS AND ART!

KATE

BETCHA THEY'RE GOOD.

PEPPER

WHY SHOULDN'T THEY BE?

ANNIE, ORPHANS

THEIR ONE MISTAKE
WAS GIVIN' UP ME!

ANNIE

SO, MAYBE NOW IT'S TIME,
AND MAYBE WHEN I WAKE,

ANNIE, ORPHANS

THEY'LL BE THERE, CALLIN' ME "BABY,"...
MAYBE.

> *(ANNIE carries MOLLY, who has fallen asleep, back to bed, and tucks her
> in as the ORPHANS, one by one, say goodnight. The MUSIC continues
> softly, underneath. ANNIE is still thinking about her parents)*

ANNIE

BETCHA HE READS.
BETCHA SHE SEWS.
MAYBE SHE'S MADE ME
A CLOSET OF CLOTHES!

MAYBE THEY'RE STRICT,
AS STRAIGHT[15] AS A LINE.
DON'T REALLY CARE,
AS LONG AS THEY'RE MINE!

SO, MAYBE NOW THIS PRAYER'S
THE LAST ONE OF ITS KIND.
> *(At the foot of the bed)*
WON'T YOU PLEASE COME GET YOUR "BABY,"...
> *(Climbs into bed. Tucks herself in.*

> *The LIGHTS dim. In the dark, we hear the song end)*

ANNIE, ORPHANS

MAYBE?

#4   *Annie's Escape*   *(Orchestra)*

> *(A faraway CHURCH BELL chimes four a.m. ANNIE goes up to the win-
> dow looking out into the street, then returns to her bed and starts
> putting some things into a small basket. The ORPHANS are dimly seen,
> waking up as ANNIE turns on a flashlight)*

PEPPER

Now what?

KATE

Annie, whatta ya doin'?

---

[15] **straight:** rigid or stern

ANNIE

Runnin' away.

TESSIE

Oh my goodness.

ANNIE

(Puts on her sweater)

My folks are never comin' for me. I gotta go find them.

JULY

Annie, you're crazy. Miss Hannigan'll catch you.

TESSIE

And give you the paddle.[16]

ANNIE

I don't care. I'm gettin' outta here.
> *(With a basket under her arm)*

Okay. I'm ready. Wish me luck.

ALL EXCEPT PEPPER

Good luck, Annie.

PEPPER

So long, dumbbell. And good luck.

> *(With the basket under her arm and shining the flashlight in front of her, ANNIE sneaks on tiptoe across the stage, toward the front door. Suspenseful MUSIC underneath. As ANNIE reaches to open the door, MISS HANNIGAN, wearing a bathrobe, flings open her door and, witch-like, stands bathed in white light before ANNIE)*

MISS HANNIGAN

Aha! Caught you!

> *(Flings ANNIE to the floor[17] and switches on the hallway light.*
>
> *LIGHTS brighten)*

Get up. Get up!

---

[16] **give you the paddle:** slang for "beat you with a paddle"

[17] **Actor's note:** Again, ANNIE should at all times be in control of the situation. MISS HANNIGAN should grab ANNIE'S arm and ANNIE should then fling herself to the floor to complete the illusion.

ANNIE
(Getting up, warily[18])
Yes, Miss Hannigan.

MISS HANNIGAN

Turn around.

(ANNIE doesn't)

I said turn around.

(ANNIE turns around and MISS HANNIGAN hits her on the backside with a paddle[19])

There! Now, what do you say? What... do... you... say?

ANNIE
(Reluctantly; through her teeth)
I love you, Miss Hannigan.

MISS HANNIGAN

Rotten orphan.

ANNIE
(Angrily)
I'm not an orphan. My mother and father left a note saying they loved me and they were coming back for me.

MISS HANNIGAN

That was 1922; this is 1933.[20]
(Switches on the LIGHT in the dormitory, sticks her head through the door and BLOWS her whistle)
Get up! Now, for this one's shenanigans,[21] you'll all get down on your knobby little knees and clean this dump until it shines like the top of the Chrysler Building![22]

---

[18] **warily:** cautiously or suspiciously

[19] **Actor's note:** MISS HANNIGAN should touch ANNIE lightly on the backside with the paddle; ANNIE should react as if she is in physical pain. MISS HANNIGAN should never actually strike ANNIE with the paddle!

[20] **Actor's note:** This line is important in that it defines for the audience the historical setting of the musical. It also tells them ANNIE is 11 years old.

[21] **shenanigans:** slang for "tricks"

[22] Completed in 1930 and considered by many to be New York City's quintessential skyscraper, the Chrysler Building was for a brief time the tallest building in the world, until the Empire State Building was completed in 1931. The Art Deco-style building is distinguished by its shiny stainless steel cap and spire (hence the reference in the script).

TESSIE

(Starting to cry)

But it's four o'clock in the morning.

MISS HANNIGAN

(Laughs cruelly)

Get to work.

ANNIE, ORPHANS

Yes, Miss Hannigan.

MISS HANNIGAN

Now!

(ORPHANS run for pails and return to front)

Why any kid would want to be an orphan, I'll never know.

#5	*Hard-Knock Life*	*(Annie, Orphans)*

(See p. 110 for music)

(As MISS HANNIGAN EXITS, slamming the door behind her, the ORPHANS throw down their scrub brushes)

ALL ORPHANS

IT'S THE HARD-KNOCK[23] LIFE FOR US!

IT'S THE HARD-KNOCK LIFE FOR US!

ANNIE

'STEADA[24] TREATED,

ALL ORPHANS

WE GET TRICKED!

---

[23] **hard-knock:** slang for "difficult" or "rough"

[24] **'steada:** "instead of"

ANNIE

'STEADA KISSES,

ALL ORPHANS

WE GET KICKED!
IT'S THE HARD-KNOCK LIFE!
GOT NO FOLKS TO SPEAK OF, SO,
IT'S THE HARD-KNOCK ROW[25] WE HOE!

ANNIE

COTTON BLANKETS,

ALL ORPHANS

'STEADA WOOL!

ANNIE

EMPTY BELLIES,

ALL ORPHANS

'STEADA FULL!
IT'S THE HARD-KNOCK LIFE!

ANNIE

DON'T IT FEEL LIKE THE WIND
IS ALWAYS HOWLIN'?

KATE, TESSIE

DON'T IT SEEM LIKE THERE'S
NEVER ANY LIGHT?

DUFFY, JULY

ONCE A DAY, DON'T YOU WANNA
THROW THE TOWEL IN?[26]

MOLLY, PEPPER

IT'S EASIER THAN PUTTIN' UP A FIGHT.

---

[25] **row:** a group of plants, planted in a line

[26] **throw the towel in:** slang for "give up" or "give in"

ANNIE
NO ONE'S THERE WHEN YOUR DREAMS
AT NIGHT GET CREEPY!

MOLLY
NO ONE CARES IF YOU GROW
OR IF YOU SHRINK!

TESSIE
NO ONE DRIES WHEN YOUR EYES
GET WET AN' WEEPY!

ALL ORPHANS
FROM THE CRYIN', YOU WOULD
THINK THIS PLACE'D SINK!
OHHHH!!!!

EMPTY-BELLY LIFE!
ROTTEN, SMELLY LIFE!
FULL-OF-SORROW LIFE!
NO-TOMORROW LIFE!

MOLLY
SANTA CLAUS, WE NEVER SEE.

PEPPER
"SANTA CLAUS," WHAT'S THAT? WHO'S HE?

ALL ORPHANS
NO ONE CARES FOR YOU A SMIDGE[27]
WHEN YOU'RE IN AN ORPHANAGE!
IT'S THE HARD-KNOCK LIFE!

MOLLY
(Making a WHISTLING SOUND and imitating MISS HANNIGAN)
You'll stay up till this dump shines like the top of the Chrysler Building.

ALL EXCEPT MOLLY
YANK THE WHISKERS FROM HER CHIN.
JAB HER WITH A SAFETY PIN.
MAKE HER DRINK A MICKEY FINN.[28]

---

[27] **smidge:** short version of **smidgen**, which is slang for "a tiny amount"

[28] **Mickey Finn:** an alcoholic drink drugged to incapacitate its consumer

I LOVE YOU, MISS HANNIGAN!

(Orchestral interlude while ANNIE and the ORPHANS finish the cleaning and strip the beds. MOLLY continues her imitation of MISS HANNIGAN)

MOLLY

(WHISTLE)

Get to work!

(WHISTLE)

Strip them beds!

(WHISTLE)

I said get to work!

(Mimes taking a flask[29] out of a pocket and taking a drink)

ALL EXCEPT MOLLY

IT'S THE HARD-KNOCK LIFE FOR US!

MOLLY

(Drunkenly)

Merry Christmas.

ALL EXCEPT MOLLY

IT'S THE HARD-KNOCK LIFE FOR US!

MOLLY

Merry Christmas.

ALL EXCEPT MOLLY

NO ONE CARES FOR YOU A SMIDGE

MOLLY

Merry Christmas.

ALL EXCEPT MOLLY

WHEN YOU'RE IN AN ORPHANAGE!

---

[29] **flask:** a flat, relatively thin container for holding liquor

*(MOLLY falls into the laundry hamper and is covered with
sheets the children have stripped from the beds)*

ALL EXCEPT MOLLY

IT'S THE HARD-KNOCK LIFE,
IT'S THE HARD-KNOCK LIFE,
IT'S THE HARD-KNOCK LIFE!

*(MISS HANNIGAN comes in, now dressed, and WHISTLES. ANNIE
and the ORPHANS run to their line-up in front of their beds, but
ANNIE'S attention remains on the laundry. SHE is hatching an
idea)*

MISS HANNIGAN

Good morning, children.

ORPHANS

Good morning, Miss Hannigan.

MISS HANNIGAN

Well?

ORPHANS

I love you, Miss Hannigan.

MOLLY

(From the hamper)
I love you, Miss Hannigan.

MISS HANNIGAN

You. What are you doing in there?

MOLLY

Nothin'.

MISS HANNIGAN

(To JULY, who is nearest the hamper)
Get her out of there!
(To MOLLY)
Your days are numbered.
(WHISTLE)
All right. Breakfast.

ORPHANS

(Dejected)

Hot mush?[30] Yuck!

MISS HANNIGAN

No, not hot mush.

(The ORPHANS and ANNIE react happily to this news)

Cold mush.

(The ORPHANS and ANNIE groan)

And after your mush, you'll go to your sewing machines. There's an order of dresses to finish, if you have to work straight through to midnight.[31]

ANNIE, ORPHANS

Yes, Miss Hannigan.

MISS HANNIGAN

Now line up.

(The ORPHANS and ANNIE file past MISS HANNIGAN, who inspects them as the laundry man, BUNDLES McCLOSKEY, ENTERS, carrying a load of clean sheets)

BUNDLES

Laundry. Laundry man.

ANNIE, ORPHANS

Mornin', Bundles.

BUNDLES

Mornin', kids. Clean sheets once a month, whether you need 'em or not.

---

[30] **mush:** a porridge made of cornmeal boiled in water or milk

[31] Child labor laws existed in some states as early as 1912, but were aimed at mining and factory work. In 1933, there was no minimum wage and children were commonly used for all other types of work, including the domestic work described here. The Fair Labor Standards Act, passed in 1938, set a minimum age for workers (16) and established a minimum wage.

(During the following, ANNIE, hidden by the ORPHANS, gets into the laundry bag)

Hey, hey, hey, Aggie. How's the prettiest gal south of 14th Street?

MISS HANNIGAN

Bundles, get out of here with that laundry!

BUNDLES

(CROSSING and picking up the laundry bag with ANNIE in it)

So long, gorgeous — and Merry Christmas.

MISS HANNIGAN

(Checking floor)

Huh, you call this clean, Annie. This place is like a pigsty[32]... Annie? Annie?

ORPHANS

Annie ain't here.

MISS HANNIGAN

What do you mean "Annie ain't here"?

TESSIE

She just went. With Mr. Bundles.

MOLLY

In the laundry bag.

MISS HANNIGAN

Bundles!

(Runs out)

Police! Police!

#6   ***Hard-Knock Life — Reprise***[33]   ***(Orphans)***

(See p. 113 for music)

(The ORPHANS cheer ANNIE'S escape)

JULY

No more hard-knock life for Annie!

---

[32] **pigsty:** a place where pigs are kept; slang for a place that is dirty or very untidy

[33] **reprise:** a return to earlier musical material — in this case, the song "Hard-Knock Life"

(The ORPHANS cheer again)
LUCKY DUCK, SHE GOT AWAY,

MOLLY
BUT WE'RE GONNA HAVE TO PAY.

KATE, TESSIE
GONNA GET OUR FACES SLAPPED.

DUFFY, PEPPER
GONNA GET OUR KNUCKLES RAPPED.[34]

ALL
IT'S THE HARD-KNOCK LIFE,
IT'S THE HARD-KNOCK LIFE,
IT'S THE HARD-KNOCK LIFE!

(BLACKOUT[35])

END OF SCENE ONE

#7	*Scene Change*	*(Orchestra)*

---

[34] **rap:** to strike sharply and quickly, usually as a form of punishment

[35] **blackout:** the sudden extinguishing of all stage lights to mark the end of a scene or an act

SCENE TWO

(LIGHTS UP.[36]

A few garbage cans place us on a street corner at St. Marks Place.[37]

It is a chilly December afternoon, a few hours later.

A DOGCATCHER with a rope runs across to STAGE RIGHT. An APPLE SELLER ENTERS, appealing to the occasional passers-by)

APPLE SELLER

Apples, apples. Two for a nickel.[38]

ANNIE

(Runs out from behind a tenement[39])
Excuse me, sir, but could you donate an apple to the orphan's picnic?

APPLE SELLER

(Giving ANNIE an apple)
Why not? Nobody's buying 'em anyway.

ANNIE

Gee thanks, Mister.

APPLE SELLER

Say kid, when is the orphan's picnic?

---

[36] In other words, the stage lights come on again.

[37] **St. Marks Place:** located in Manhattan in the area known as the East Village, this street is named for the nearby St. Mark's Church-in-the-Bowery, one of New York's oldest places of worship. In the 1930s, the street was one of the more depressed areas of the city. In more recent times, the street became a home to the hippies of the 1960s and the punk culture of the 1970s and 1980s. Today, it's still a gritty center for New York's rebellious young people.

[38] During the Depression, many people tried to make money by selling apples on the street. There was a glut of agricultural goods (meaning there were far more goods produced than people wanted or needed), which explains why apples were readily available to sell, and why they were sold at such a low price.

[39] **tenement:** an apartment building, usually rundown and low-rent

ANNIE

(Smiling and taking a big bite of the apple)

Soon as I take a bite.

(The APPLE SELLER shakes his head at having been conned by a child and wanders OFFSTAGE in search of customers. The SOUND of barking dogs is heard from OFFSTAGE and a DOGCATCHER ENTERS UPSTAGE RIGHT, pushing a wheeled dog cage lettered "N.Y.C. Dog Pound".[40]

The DOGCATCHER CROSSES to CENTERSTAGE, looking for stray dogs. HE speaks to ANNIE)

DOGCATCHER

You seen any stray mutts around here?

ANNIE

No, sir.

DOGCATCHER

Good. Then they must all be runnin' wild over to Astor Place.[41]

(The DOGCATCHER EXITS STAGE LEFT; ANNIE watches him go and then turns and notices a DOG OFFSTAGE RIGHT)

ANNIE

Hey, there's one they didn't get.

(ANNIE gets down on her hands and knees and signals for the DOG to come to her; SANDY, crawling, ENTERS from STAGE RIGHT and CROSSES to ANNIE. NOTE: SANDY should be played by an actor... a human actor, that is.

To SANDY)

They're after you, ain't they? Well, they're after me, too. But don't worry, I ain't gonna let them get you or me.

---

[40] **dog pound:** a public place where stray dogs are held (or "impounded")

[41] **Astor Place:** a street adjacent to St. Marks Place, named after the wealthy Astor family. John Jacob Astor was a fur trader who made his fortune at the beginning of the nineteenth century, becoming the richest man of his time in the United States. In the nineteenth century, the area was a home to some of New York's most elite families. It was also the site of New York's first free library.

#8   *Tomorrow*   *(Annie, Sandy)*

(See p. 114 for music)

Everything's gonna be fine. For the both of us. If not today, well...

THE SUN'LL COME OUT
TOMORROW.
BET YOUR BOTTOM DOLLAR[42]
THAT TOMORROW,
THERE'LL BE SUN!

JUST THINKIN' ABOUT
TOMORROW
CLEARS AWAY THE COBWEBS
AND THE SORROW,
'TIL THERE'S NONE!

WHEN I'M STUCK WITH A DAY
THAT'S GRAY
AND LONELY,
I JUST STICK OUT MY CHIN
AND GRIN
AND SAY,
"OH,

THE SUN'LL COME OUT
TOMORROW,
SO YA GOTTA HANG ON
'TIL TOMORROW,
COME WHAT MAY."

TOMORROW!

SANDY

TOMORROW!

ANNIE

I LOVE YA,

SANDY

TOMORROW!

---

[42] **bet your bottom dollar**: an expression indicating certainty; refers to something
so certain that you'd be safe betting your last dollar on it

ANNIE

YOU'RE ALWAYS A DAY AWAY!

(A POLICEMAN, LT. WARD, ENTERS)

WARD

Hey, you! Little girl. Come here.

ANNIE

Yes, Officer?

WARD

That dog there. Ain't he a stray?[43]

ANNIE

A stray? Oh, no, Officer. He's my dog.

WARD

Your dog, huh? So, what's his name?

ANNIE

His name? His name is... Sandy. Right, that's it. I call him Sandy because of his nice sandy color.

WARD

Okay, let's see him answer to his name.

ANNIE

Well, you see, Officer... I just got him and sometimes...

WARD

Call him!

ANNIE

Here, Sandy. Here, boy. Sandy.

(SANDY crosses to ANNIE, stands and puts his front paws on her chest)

Good Sandy. Good old Sandy.

---

[43] Meaning a **stray** dog (a dog that is lost and/or wandering around)

WARD

Next time you take him out, I wanna see him on a leash and with a
license,[44] or else he goes to the pound.

ANNIE

Yes, sir. I understand.

WARD

Now get along with you before you catch your death[45] of cold in this
weather.

ANNIE

Oh, I don't mind the weather.
> WHEN I'M STUCK WITH A DAY
> THAT'S GRAY
> AND LONELY,
> I JUST STICK OUT MY CHIN
> AND GRIN
> AND SAY,
> "OH,
>
> THE SUN'LL COME OUT
> TOMORROW,
> SO YA GOTTA HANG ON
> 'TIL TOMORROW,
> COME WHAT MAY."
> TOMORROW!

SANDY

TOMORROW!

ANNIE

I LOVE YA,

SANDY

TOMORROW!

ANNIE

YOU'RE ALWAYS A DAY AWAY.

---

[44] **license:** proof of official or legal permission to own something, such as a dog

[45] **to catch your death:** an expression meaning — what else? — "to die"

TOMORROW!

SANDY

TOMORROW!

ANNIE

I LOVE YA,

SANDY

TOMORROW!

ANNIE

YOU'RE ALWAYS A DAY AWAY!

(ANNIE and SANDY walk behind a tenement and disappear from sight.

BLACKOUT)

END OF SCENE TWO

#9	*Scene Change*	*(Orchestra)*

SCENE THREE

(The LIGHTS come up as MISS HANNIGAN goes into her office, which contains a desk, a rocking chair, and a rolling office chair. On the desk is a cathedral-style radio.[46] TESSIE runs in from STAGE LEFT and goes up to MISS HANNIGAN)

#10	*Little Girls*	*(Miss Hannigan)*

(See p. 116 for music)

TESSIE

Miss Hannigan, you know your souvenir pillow from Coney Island?[47]

MISS HANNIGAN

Yeah.

TESSIE

Molly just threw up on it.

(MISS HANNIGAN threatens TESSIE. TESSIE runs off STAGE LEFT; MISS HANNIGAN sits in the office chair. SHE gets up, holding a broken doll on which she has just sat)

MISS HANNIGAN

LITTLE GIRLS,
LITTLE GIRLS...
EVERYWHERE I TURN,
I CAN SEE THEM.
LITTLE GIRLS,
LITTLE GIRLS...
NIGHT AND DAY
I EAT, SLEEP AND BREATHE THEM.

SOME WOMEN ARE DRIPPING WITH DIAMONDS,
SOME WOMEN ARE DRIPPING WITH PEARLS.
LUCKY ME!
LUCKY ME!
LOOK AT WHAT I'M DRIPPING WITH:
LITTLE GIRLS!

---

[46] a 1930s-style radio receiver which in shape resembled the arches of a gothic cathedral

[47] **Coney Island:** a section of Brooklyn, New York that sits on the Atlantic Ocean. A popular tourist spot since the mid-1800s, Coney Island is still known for its amusement park (featuring the world-famous Cyclone roller coaster, built in 1927), its boardwalk, its beaches and the New York Aquarium.

SOMEDAY I'LL STEP ON THEIR FRECKLES.
SOME NIGHT I'LL STRAIGHTEN THEIR CURLS.
SEND A FLOOD,
SEND THE FLU —
ANYTHING THAT
YOU CAN DO
TO LITTLE GIRLS!

(PEPPER and DUFFY have been playing cards and a fight erupts. We hear PEPPER saying "You cheated." DUFFY answers "I did not," and PEPPER responds with "You did too," over and over. The other ORPHANS gather around, encouraging the fight. MISS HANNIGAN crosses the hall, opens the door and BLOWS the whistle)

Shut up!

(SHE returns to her office and collapses into her rocking chair. OFFICER WARD ENTERS from the street, dragging ANNIE by the collar. ANNIE points out MISS HANNIGAN'S door to WARD and HE knocks.

MISS HANNIGAN responds to the knock)
Yeah. Come in.

(As WARD ENTERS MISS HANNIGAN'S office, ANNIE crosses the hall to greet the ORPHANS)

WARD
Good afternoon. Miss Hannigan, is it?

MISS HANNIGAN
Yeah.

WARD
I'm Lt. Ward of the 17th Precinct. We found your runaway.

MISS HANNIGAN
Oh, thank you, Officer.[48]

---

[48] **Actor's note:** MISS HANNIGAN is playing the saint so WARD will not see how terribly she treats the orphans.

WARD

She was in one of them[49] Hoovervilles[50] over to the river. With a bunch of bums.[51]

A typical Hooverville of the period.

ANNIE

They weren't bums.

WARD

Had a mangy[52] mutt with her, but he got away.

MISS HANNIGAN

Oh, poor punkin', out in the freezin' cold with just that thin sweater. I hope you didn't catch influenza.[53] Thanks so much again, Officer.

WARD

All in the line of duty.
> *(To ANNIE)*

And you. Don't let me ever hear that you run away again. From this nice lady.
> *(To MISS HANNIGAN with a little salute)*

Good afternoon.

MISS HANNIGAN

Good afternoon, Officer.
> *(Sees WARD out, then REENTERS her office)[54]*

The next time you walk out that door, it'll be 1953. Well, are you glad to be back? Huh?

---

[49] **one of them:** "one of those"; WARD'S grammar is far from perfect!

[50] **Hoovervilles:** ramshackle shantytowns that sprang up all over the nation during the Depression to house the huge numbers of homeless Americans. These "villages," which consisted of primitive shelters made of packing boxes and bits of scrap metal, were called "Hoovervilles" in ironic reference to President Herbert Hoover, who many thought responsible for the Depression and their plight.

[51] **bum:** a tramp or vagrant (someone who moves from place to place without a permanent home or way of making a living)

[52] **mangy:** filthy, dirty or shabby; refers to **mange**, a skin disease caused by mites and characterized by skin lesions, itching and loss of hair

[53] **influenza:** a serious and contagious viral infection in which the respiratory tract becomes inflamed. Symptoms include fever, chills, muscular pain and general weakness.

[54] **Actor's note:** as soon as she sees WARD out, MISS HANNIGAN returns to her old mean self.

ANNIE

(Cowed [55]; reluctantly)

Yes, Miss Hannigan.

MISS HANNIGAN

Liar! What's the one thing I always taught you: never tell a lie.

(Grabs ANNIE around the shoulders, tossing her from side to side. [56]

GRACE FARRELL ENTERS, carrying an attachè case [57])

GRACE

Good afternoon. Miss Hannigan?

MISS HANNIGAN

Yes?

GRACE

I'm Grace Farrell, private secretary to Oliver Warbucks.

(Sits in the office chair, STAGE LEFT of the desk)

MISS HANNIGAN

The Oliver Warbucks? The millionaire?

GRACE

Mr. Warbucks has decided to invite an orphan to spend the Christmas holidays at his home.

MISS HANNIGAN

What sort of orphan did he have in mind?

GRACE

Well, she should be friendly.

(ANNIE waves to GRACE)

And intelligent.

---

[55] **cowed:** threatened, intimidated

[56] **Actor's note:** Again, safety first! MISS HANNIGAN should grab ANNIE by the shoulders and try to hold her in place while ANNIE thrashes around from side to side. ANNIE is always in control, but it will appear to the audience as if MISS HANNIGAN is shaking her.

[57] **attachè case:** a thin, hinged briefcase, with flat sides and a lock

ANNIE

Mississippi. Capital M-I-double-S-I-double-S-I-double-P-I. Mississippi.

GRACE

And cheerful.

> *(ANNIE laughs)*

MISS HANNIGAN

> *(Kicks ANNIE to quiet her [58])*

You shut up. And how old?

GRACE

Oh, age doesn't really matter. Oh, say, eight or nine.

> *(ANNIE gestures upward to indicate she wants GRACE to say a
> higher age)*

Ten.

> *(ANNIE gestures still higher)*

Eleven.

> *(ANNIE gestures to GRACE to stop and then points to her own
> hair)*

Yes, eleven would be perfect. And oh, I almost forgot: Mr. Warbucks prefers
red-headed children.

MISS HANNIGAN

Eleven? A red-head? Sorry, we don't have any orphans like that.

GRACE

What about this child right here?

---

[58] **Actor's note:** a light tap with the foot will suffice. ANNIE can register pain to
complete the illusion.

*(MISS HANNIGAN rushes in between GRACE and ANNIE and pins [59]
ANNIE behind her back)*

MISS HANNIGAN

Annie? Oh, no! You don't want her.

GRACE

Annie, would you like to spend the next two weeks at Mr. Warbucks' house?

ANNIE

I would love to.

MISS HANNIGAN

You can have any orphan here, but not Annie.

GRACE

Perhaps I should call the Board of Orphans[60] and...

(MISS HANNIGAN laughs)

MISS HANNIGAN

If it's Annie you want, it's Annie you get.

GRACE

It's Annie I want.

ANNIE

Oh, boy!

GRACE

If you'll get her coat, I'll take her along right now.

MISS HANNIGAN

She don't have no coat.[61]

GRACE

Then we'll buy her one.

---

[59] **pin:** to hold fast and keep from moving

[60] **Board of Orphans:** the city agency in charge of making sure orphans are properly cared for; in other words, MISS HANNIGAN'S bosses!

[61] "She doesn't have a coat." MISS HANNIGAN'S grammar is not very good either.

ANNIE

Oh, boy!

GRACE

Come along, Annie. Mr. Warbucks' limousine[62] is outside.

ANNIE

Oh, boy! I can hardly believe it.

MISS HANNIGAN

She can hardly believe it?

> (GRACE and ANNIE start to leave. The ORPHANS gather around
> ANNIE in the hallway)

ANNIE

Hey kids, I'm getting out for Christmas. I'll write to ya.

#11	*Little Girls — Reprise*	*(Miss Hannigan)*

(See p. 117 for music)

> (ANNIE and the ORPHANS say goodbye. As GRACE and ANNIE
> EXIT, the ORPHANS run past MISS HANNIGAN, screaming and
> cheering. THEY EXIT STAGE RIGHT)

MISS HANNIGAN

SOMEDAY I'LL LAND IN THE NUTHOUSE[63]
WITH ALL THE NUTS AND THE SQUIRRELS.
THERE I'LL STAY,

---

[62] **limousine:** a large, luxurious automobile, usually with a private driver (or "**chauffeur**")

[63] **nuthouse:** slang for "mental hospital"

TUCKED AWAY
'TIL THE PROHIBITION[64] OF LITTLE GIRLS!

(BLACKOUT)

END OF SCENE THREE

| #12 | *Scene Change* | *(Orchestra)* |

---

[64] **prohibition:** a law or command that forbids something (in this case, the existence of "little girls"); this is also a reference to the "era of prohibition" from 1920-1933 when the manufacture, sale and transport of alcoholic beverages was outlawed in the United States by the Eighteenth Amendment to the Constitution. Opponents to this Amendment argued that the prohibition of liquor was an unnecessary restriction of personal choice, and the prohibition of liquor was repealed (undone) by the Twenty-first Amendment in 1933.

SCENE FOUR

(LIGHTS up.

The living room of the WARBUCKS mansion.[65]

A couple of hours later.

DRAKE, the English butler,[66] *is supervising the work of the SERVANTS of the house, who are bustling about at work: CECILLE*[67] *and ANNETTE, a pair of French maids; MRS. GREER, the housekeeper; MRS. PUGH,*[68] *the cook, standing with pad and pen writing out a menu; and FOUR MANSERVANTS.*[69]

GRACE FARRELL and ANNIE ENTER through the door. ANNIE is wearing a new hat and a new fur-collared coat)

DRAKE
Good afternoon, Miss Farrell.

GRACE
Good afternoon, Drake. Everyone.

SERVANTS
Good afternoon, Miss.

GRACE
Has Mr. Warbucks arrived yet?

DRAKE
No, Miss. We're expecting him any minute.

ANNIE
Do you really live here, or is this a train station?

---

[65] **mansion:** a large, dignified house, usually for the very wealthy

[66] **butler:** the head servant in a household

[67] **Cecille:** pronounced "Suh-seel"

[68] **Pugh:** pronounced "Pyoo"

[69] **manservant:** a male servant

GRACE

We really live here.
> (*To SERVANTS*)

Now, would you all come here for a moment, please?

DRAKE

Quickly everyone.

GRACE

This is Annie. She'll be with us for Christmas.
> (*To ANNIE*)

Annie, this is everyone.

ANNIE

Hi, everyone.

DRAKE

May I take your coat, Miss?

ANNIE

Will I get it back?

GRACE

Of course, dear. Now, what do you want to do first?

ANNIE

The floors. I'll scrub them first; then I'll get to the windows.

GRACE

Annie, you won't have to do any cleaning. You're our guest.

#13   *I Think I'm Gonna Like It Here*   **(Annie, Grace, Servants)**

(See p. 118 for music)

And, for the next two weeks, you're going to have a swell time. Now...

CECILLE WILL PICK OUT ALL YOUR CLOTHES.

CECILLE

Green is her best color; no, blue, I think.

GRACE

YOUR BATH IS DRAWN[70] BY MRS. GREER.

---

[70] **to draw a bath:** to prepare the water for a bath

MRS. GREER

Soap... no, bubbles, I think.

GRACE

ANNETTE COMES IN TO MAKE YOUR BED.

ANNETTE

The silk; no, the satin sheets, I think.

ANNIE

I THINK I'M GONNA LIKE IT HERE!

GRACE, SERVANTS

WHEN YOU WAKE,
RING FOR DRAKE.
DRAKE WILL BRING YOUR TRAY.
WHEN YOU'RE THROUGH,
MRS. PUGH
COMES TO TAKE IT AWAY.

GRACE, SERVANTS

NO NEED TO PICK UP ANY TOYS.

ANNIE

That's okay, I haven't got any, anyway!

GRACE

NO FINGER WILL YOU LIFT, MY DEAR.

GRACE, SERVANTS

WE HAVE BUT ONE REQUEST:
PLEASE, PUT US TO THE TEST.

ANNIE

I KNOW I'M GONNA LIKE IT HERE.

USED TO ROOM
IN A TOMB,
WHERE I'D SIT AND FREEZE.
GET ME NOW.
HOLY COW!
COULD SOMEONE PINCH ME, PLEASE?

(A SERVANT pinches ANNIE.[71] *ANNIE reacts)*

GRACE

She didn't mean it.

WE'VE NEVER HAD A LITTLE GIRL.

SERVANTS

WE'VE NEVER HAD A LITTLE GIRL.

ANNIE

I'M VERY GLAD TO VOLUNTEER.

GRACE, SERVANTS

WE HOPE YOU UNDERSTAND
YOUR WISH IS OUR COMMAND.

ANNIE

I KNOW I'M GONNA LIKE IT HERE.

GRACE, SERVANTS

(Simultaneously)
WE KNOW YOU'RE GONNA LIKE IT HERE.

ALL

(Spoken)
WELCOME!

(As the APPLAUSE dies, a voice is heard from OFFSTAGE RIGHT)

WARBUCKS

(OFFSTAGE)
Where is everybody?

(OLIVER WARBUCKS, trailed by a uniformed CHAUFFEUR,[72] *comes
bustling in. WARBUCKS is carrying a bulging briefcase and the
CHAUFFEUR is carrying two suitcases. WARBUCKS takes off his
overcoat*[73] *and hands it to DRAKE)*

---

[71] **Actor's note:** The SERVANT should only pretend to pinch ANNIE, and let ANNIE react as if she
has actually been pinched.

[72] **chauffeur:** a private driver

[73] **overcoat:** a heavy coat worn over other clothing in times of cold weather

Hello, everybody.

SERVANTS

Sir.

GRACE

Welcome home, Mr. Warbucks.

WARBUCKS

It's good to be home.

DRAKE

How was your flight from Chicago?

WARBUCKS

Not bad... only took eleven hours.[74] Grace?

GRACE

(Eagerly)

Yes, sir?

WARBUCKS

Messages?

GRACE

(Consulting a notepad)

President Roosevelt[75] wants you to call him at the White House.

President Franklin Delano Roosevelt.

---

[74] **Actor's note:** Today the flight from Chicago to New York takes only two to three hours. This line will probably get laughs from the audience, so be prepared!

[75] President Franklin Delano Roosevelt was thirty-second President of the United States, serving from 1933 to his death in 1945. He was born to a wealthy family and had every advantage money, education and social position can buy. But he also knew great suffering as a result of a bout of polio which left him paralyzed for half of his life. He is best remembered for the many social programs instituted by his administration to lessen the harmful effects of the Depression. These social and economic programs greatly expanded the role of the United States government in the lives of its citizens.

WARBUCKS

I'll get back to him tomorrow.[76]

GRACE

(Trying to introduce ANNIE to WARBUCKS)
Mr. Warbucks...

WARBUCKS

All right, good to see you all again.

SERVANTS

Sir.

WARBUCKS

Drake, dismiss the staff.

DRAKE

Yes, sir.

(The SERVANTS, not including GRACE, EXIT; WARBUCKS turns to speak to GRACE and, for the first time, notices ANNIE)

WARBUCKS

And, Grace, if you'll get your notebook... Who is that?

GRACE

This is Annie, Mr. Warbucks: the orphan who will be with us for Christmas.

WARBUCKS

That's not a boy. Orphans are boys.

GRACE

I'm sorry, sir, you just said "orphan". So, I chose a girl.

WARBUCKS

Well, I suppose she'll have to do.
(Frowningly approaching ANNIE, assessing[77] her)
Annie, huh? Annie what?

---

[76] Note to WARBUCKS: this line is an indication of WARBUCKS' wealth and power; even the
President of the United States is of secondary importance to him!

[77] **assess:** to look over or evaluate

ANNIE

(Nervously)

Oh, I'm just Annie, Mr. Warbucks, sir. I haven't got any last name. I'm sorry I'm not a boy.

WARBUCKS

(Obviously not meaning it)

Not at all. I couldn't be happier. Grace, we'll start with the figures on the iron-ore[78] shipments from... Toledo[79] to...

(Made uncomfortable by the presence of ANNIE, aside[80] to GRACE)

What are we supposed to do with this child?

GRACE

(Aside to WARBUCKS)

It *is* her first night here, sir.

WARBUCKS

(Aside to GRACE)

Hmm.

(To ANNIE)

Well, Annie, I guess we ought to do something special on your first night.

(Has an idea)

Would you like to go to a movie?[81]

ANNIE

(Checking GRACE to see if this would be all right; GRACE nods "yes")

Gosh, Mr. Warbucks, I've never been to one.

---

[78] **ore:** a mineral or combination of minerals which can be processed to produce a valuable material, especially a metal (in this case, iron)

[79] **Toledo:** a city in northwest Ohio, on Lake Erie

[80] **aside:** a remark made softly, so people close by will not hear — in this case, WARBUCKS makes an aside to GRACE, which ANNIE is not meant to hear. WARBUCKS should lower his voice when he speaks, and ANNIE should pretend she doesn't hear. He should always speak loud enough for the audience to hear, though.

[81] The 1930s are considered the "golden age" of the Hollywood studio film. Sound had been introduced in late 1927, and by the 1930s movie audiences found escape from the misery of the Depression in musicals, westerns, adventure films, gangster movies and screwball comedies starring such actors as Greta Garbo, Mae West, Betty Davis, Katharine Hepburn, Cary Grant, Gary Cooper, Clark Gable, James Stewart, James Cagney, Fred Astaire and Ginger Rogers.

WARBUCKS

Then you'll go to the Roxy.[82] And then an ice-cream soda at Rumpelmayer's[83] and a hansom[84] cab ride around Central Park.[85]

ANNIE

Golly!

WARBUCKS

Grace, forget about the dictation for tonight. Instead, you take Annie to the movies.

GRACE

Yes, sir.

ANNIE

(Obviously disappointed about something)

Aw, gee.

WARBUCKS

Something the matter, Annie?

ANNIE

It's just that... well... I thought *you* were going to take me.

WARBUCKS

Oh, no, I'm afraid I'll be far too busy tonight.

ANNIE

Aw, gee.

---

[82] The Roxy Music Hall, one of the great movie theatres of the era; such theatres were so ornate and spectacular they became known as "movie palaces."

[83] A famous ice cream parlor on Central Park in New York City

[84] **hansom cab:** a two-wheeled covered carriage (pulled by a horse) on which the driver's seat is located above and behind the passenger compartment. Hansom cab rides around Central Park are still available in New York City today.

[85] **Central Park:** an 840-acre park in the center of Manhattan; Central Park is one of the first public parks designed by landscape architects, and contains numerous walks, lakes and open fields in addition to a zoo, a skating rink, an open-air theatre and the Metropolitan Museum of Art.

WARBUCKS

Now, Annie... I've just been away for six weeks. And when a man is running a multi-billion-dollar corporation...

ANNIE

Oh, sure. I know. That's okay, Mr. Warbucks.

WARBUCKS

(Regards [86] ANNIE and is moved by her disappointment; calls OFFSTAGE LEFT)

Drake!

DRAKE

(From OFFSTAGE LEFT)

Yes, sir?

WARBUCKS

Get our coats.

ANNIE

(Smiling triumphantly; she's won)

Aw, gee!

WARBUCKS

Grace, you'll come, too, of course.

(GRACE nods "yes" as DRAKE ENTERS with three coats)

DRAKE

Which car will you be wanting, sir?

WARBUCKS

The Duesenberg.[87] No, wait. This child's been cooped up in an Orphanage. We'll walk.

GRACE

Walk to the Roxy?

---

[86] **regard:** to consider

[87] **Duesenberg:** one of the grandest luxury automobiles of the era, advertised as "The World's Finest Motor Car." Today, automobile collectors pay upwards of one million dollars for a Duesenberg.

WARBUCKS

Why not? It's only 45 blocks.

GRACE

Yes, sir!

(As DRAKE helps WARBUCKS into his coat, the set begins to change to become upper Fifth Avenue.[88] WARBUCKS strolls DOWNSTAGE while GRACE and ANNIE get into their coats behind him)

WARBUCKS

Ah, smell those bus fumes![89] There's no air like the air of New York. Come on, you slowpokes! We gotta get to the Roxy before the prices change.

(LIGHTS crossfade as SCENE FOUR blends into SCENE FIVE)

END OF SCENE FOUR

---

[88] Fifth Avenue, which divides Manhattan's East Side from its West Side, is known for its elegant residences and exclusive shops. Today, many of the city's major museums are located on Fifth Avenue, as is the Empire State Building.

[89] Public buses make up one half of the New York City public transportation system. The other half consists of the subway system, an underground network of trains.

SCENE FIVE

#14   *N.Y.C.*   (*Warbucks, Grace, Annie, Star-To-Be, Chorus*)
(See p. 121 for music)

(GRACE, ANNIE and WARBUCKS begin strolling as various NEW YORKERS ENTER)

New York City's Times Square by night, c. 1933.

WARBUCKS, GRACE

N.Y.C. —
THE SHIMMER OF TIMES SQUARE,[90]

WARBUCKS

THE PULSE,

GRACE

THE BEAT,

WARBUCKS, GRACE

THE DRIVE!

WARBUCKS

N.Y.C. —
YOU MIGHT SAY THAT I'M SQUARE,
BUT WOW —!
I COME
ALIVE.

ALL

THE CITY'S BRIGHT
AS A PENNY ARCADE.[91]
IT BLINKS, IT TILTS, IT RINGS.

ANNIE

TO THINK THAT

---

[90] **Times Square:** an area in midtown Manhattan which was in 1930 (and still is today) the center of New York's famed theatre district (the many lighted marquees, billboards and electric signs gave Broadway its nickname "The Great White Way"). Times Square is also a thriving business center and popular tourist spot. It is the site of New York's annual New Year's celebration, and is often called the "Crossroads Of The World."

[91] **penny arcade:** an arcade containing machines that provide entertainment for the cost of a penny — a precursor to today's video arcades.

I'VE LIVED HERE ALL OF MY LIFE
AND NEVER SEEN THESE THINGS!

ALL

N.Y.C. —
THE WHOLE WORLD KEEPS COMING,
BY BUS,
BY TRAIN;
YOU CAN'T
EXPLAIN
THEIR YEN[92]
FOR...

STAR-TO-BE

N.Y.C. —
JUST GOT HERE THIS MORNING:
THREE BUCKS,
TWO BAGS,
ONE ME!

N.Y.C.,
I GIVE YOU FAIR WARNING:
UP THERE,
IN LIGHTS
I'LL BE![93]

ALL

GO ASK THE GERSHWINS[94]
OR KAUFMAN AND HART[95]
THE PLACE THEY LOVE THE BEST.
THOUGH CALIFORNIA
PAYS BIG FOR THEIR ART,
THEIR FAN MAIL COMES ADDRESSED

---

[92] **yen:** longing, craving

[93] Meaning the STAR-TO-BE is going to be so famous that his or her name is going to be up on a theatre marquee

[94] George and Ira Gershwin, a composer and lyricist team (they were brothers) who took Broadway by storm, then went on to write songs for Hollywood films

[95] George S. Kaufman and Moss Hart, a playwriting team who took Broadway by storm, then went on to write screenplays for Hollywood films

TO N.Y.C.
TOMORROW, A PENTHOUSE[96]
THAT'S WAY
UP HIGH…

STAR-TO-BE

TONIGHT?
THE "Y." [97]
WHY NOT?
IT'S N.Y.C.

(ALL march down to the front edge of the stage)

ALL

N.Y.C.,
YOU'RE STANDING ROOM ONLY.
YOU CROWD,
YOU CRAMP.
YOU'RE STILL
THE CHAMP!
AMEN
FOR N.Y. —

MAN
(Slamming open a brownstone[98] window)
Keep it quiet down there!

ALL

(Quietly)
— C.

---

[96] **penthouse:** a residence on the top floor (or one of the top floors) of a building; usually very expensive

[97] The Y.M.C.A. (Young Men's Christian Association), an international organization which provides athletic, recreational, cultural and educational services to its members; many Y.M.C.A.s also offer cheap housing alternatives.

[98] **brownstone:** a house built or faced with "brownstone," a brownish-red sandstone. This material was used widely during the nineteenth century on the east coast of the United States.

(As the stage begins to slowly dim, an USHERETTE [99] with a flashlight ENTERS from STAGE LEFT)

USHERETTE

Immediate seating... there is immediate seating.

(The line of people breaks up, some wander off up to the Roxy, the others EXIT STAGE LEFT and STAGE RIGHT, going about their own business)

WARBUCKS

Popcorn, what do you say to some popcorn? I haven't had popcorn since...

(ANNIE yawns and leans against WARBUCKS' SLEEVE)

GIVE IN.
DON'T FIGHT.
GOOD GIRL.
GOOD NIGHT.
SLEEP TIGHT
IN
N.Y.C.

(WARBUCKS picks the sleepy ANNIE up in his arms and walks off STAGE RIGHT. GRACE follows. Two CHILDREN run across UPSTAGE, one calling "Come on! Ma will kill us." All that is left is the COP on the beat. HE takes a final check of the Square and strolls off DOWNSTAGE LEFT. From UPSTAGE RIGHT, SANDY comes wandering in all alone. HE stops CENTERSTAGE and sits, looks STAGE RIGHT, looks STAGE LEFT, and trudges off, looking for ANNIE as the LIGHTS fade and the scene fades)

END OF SCENE FIVE

---

[99] **usherette:** a girl or woman who works in a theatre or stadium to show audience members to their seats

SCENE SIX

(LIGHTS up.

MISS HANNIGAN'S office in the Orphanage, as in SCENE THREE. MISS HANNIGAN, seated by her desk, notices the time and turns on the cathedral-style, table-model[100] Philco[101] radio)

ANNOUNCER'S VOICE

Once again we bring you the romance of Helen Trent... who sets out to prove that just because a woman is thirty-five or more, romance in life need not be over.[102]

MISS HANNIGAN

God, I hope not.

(GRACE FARRELL ENTERS)

GRACE

Good afternoon, Miss Hannigan.

MISS HANNIGAN

(Switching off the radio)
Whatsa matter, Warbucks fed up with Annie already?

GRACE

On the contrary...
(Hands MISS HANNIGAN a legal document)
Miss Hannigan, this has to be signed and sent back to the Board of Orphans no later than 10 o'clock tomorrow.

A radio from the period.

MISS HANNIGAN

What for?

---

[100] Meaning it is a small unit, designed to sit on a tabletop or on a shelf

[101] Philco was a popular American radio manufacturer of the era. It later went on to manufacture television sets.

[102] Radio was at the height of its popularity in the 1930s and 1940s, before the advent of television. During the Depression, radio programs provided listeners with a temporary escape from their worries. Radio programming consisted of live music, comedy shows (featuring the likes of Jack Benny, Burns and Allen, Ed Wynn and Amos 'n' Andy) and dramas. Soap operas like "The Romance of Helen Trent" (so called because they were primarily sponsored by soap companies) saw an explosion of popularity in 1933, the year they burst onto the national radio broadcasting scene.

GRACE

Because Mr. Warbucks is so taken with Annie that he wants to adopt her.

MISS HANNIGAN

Annie? The daughter of a millionaire?

GRACE

The daughter of a billionaire.

MISS HANNIGAN

Would you excuse me for a moment, please?
>   *(Goes out into the hallway, lets out a long, loud scream of fury and frus-*
>   *tration, then returns to the office)*

Got any more wonderful news?

GRACE

Merry Christmas, Miss Hannigan.
>   *(As GRACE EXITS, she bumps into ROOSTER)*

ROOSTER

Oops, pardon me, blondie.[103]

>   *(GRACE gives ROOSTER a disdainful look and EXITS; ROOSTER ENTERS)*

Hi ya, Sis. Long time no see.

MISS HANNIGAN

Rooster? They finally let you outta prison? What were you in for this time?

ROOSTER

Some old geezer[104] said I swindled[105] him outta eleven hundred bucks.

MISS HANNIGAN

Why'd he say that?

---

[103] **blondie:** slang for a person with blonde hair (such as GRACE)

[104] **geezer:** slang for an eccentric old man

[105] **swindle:** to cheat out of money or property

LILY

(ENTERING)

Because the Rooster swindled him outta eleven hundred bucks.

ROOSTER

Sis, I'd like you to meet a friend of mine from...

LILY

Jersey City![106]

MISS HANNIGAN

Rooster, do me a favor. Get outta here.

ROOSTER

So who was the blondie I bumped into when I come in? Looked like she had a couple of dollars.

MISS HANNIGAN

She works for Oliver Warbucks.

LILY

The Oliver Warbucks?

MISS HANNIGAN

Annie, one of the orphans from here, is gettin' adopted by him.

LILY

Crummy orphan!

ROOSTER

Yeah, livin' in the lap of luxury[107] while the two Hannigan kids ended up on the skids![108]

#15   *Easy Street*   (Rooster, Miss Hannigan, Lily)

(See p. 124 for music)

IT AIN'T FAIR
HOW WE SCROUNGE[109]

---

[106] **Jersey City:** a city in northeast New Jersey, across the Hudson River from lower Manhattan

[107] **the lap of luxury:** an expression meaning a state of great wealth and material comfort

[108] **on the skids:** bankrupt, in financial distress

[109] **scrounge:** to beg; also, to rummage around for food and supplies

FOR THREE OR FOUR BUCKS,
WHILE SHE GETS WARBUCKS.

MISS HANNIGAN

THE LITTLE BRAT!
IT AIN'T FAIR. THIS HERE LIFE
IS DRIVIN' ME NUTS!
WHILE WE GET PEANUTS,
SHE'S LIVIN' FAT!

LILY

MAYBE SHE HOLDS THE KEY,
THAT LITTLE LADY...

MISS HANNIGAN

TO GETTIN' MORE BUCKS

ROOSTER

INSTEAD OF LESS!
MAYBE WE FIX THE GAME
WITH SOMETHING SHADY...

LILY

WHERE DOES THAT PUT US?

ROOSTER

GIVE YOU ONE GUESS!

ROOSTER, MISS HANNIGAN, LILY

YES!
EASY STREET![110]
EASY STREET!
ANNIE IS THE KEY,
YES SIRREE,
YES SIRREE,
YES SIRREE,
YEAH!
EASY STREET!

---

[110] **easy street:** an expression meaning a state of financial security, wealth and independence

EASY STREET!

THAT'S WHERE WE'RE GONNA
BE!

(BLACKOUT)

END OF SCENE SIX

#16	*Scene Change*	*(Orchestra)*

SCENE SEVEN

(LIGHTS up.

WARBUCKS' office in his mansion.

Late morning of the following day.

WARBUCKS is seated at his desk, talking on the telephone. GRACE is nearby with a steno[111] pad)

WARBUCKS

(Into the phone)

Yes... Yes, Mr. President. No, I am not asking for your help, but I'm telling you that you've got to do something. All right, we'll talk about it on...

GRACE

Friday.

WARBUCKS

Friday. Listen, Mister President, why don't we bury the hatchet and you come here with Mrs. Roosevelt for supper Christmas Eve?

(Disappointed)

You will? Wonderful. Goodbye, Mister President.

(Hangs up phone)

Grace, find out what Democrats[112] eat.

GRACE

Yes, sir.

WARBUCKS

The package from Tiffany's?[113]

GRACE

Arrived this morning.

---

[111] short for "stenographer's pad". A **stenographer** is someone who is employed to take dictation, often with a special system of writing called "shorthand."

[112] **Democrat:** a member of the Democratic Party, one of the two major political organizations in the United States. ROOSEVELT was a member of the Democratic Party. WARBUCKS is a member of the Republican Party, the other major political group.

[113] **Tiffany & Co.:** a famous Fifth Avenue jeweler, now over 100 years old

WARBUCKS

Fine. I'm going to give it to her and then tell her that I want to adopt her.

GRACE

She's going to be the happiest little girl in the world.

WARBUCKS

Get her down here.

GRACE

Yes, sir.

> *(EXITS STAGE RIGHT.*
>
> *ANNIE ENTERS. SHE is now dressed in a red dress and her hair is curled to look for the first time as she does in "Little Orphan Annie.")*

ANNIE

Hello.

WARBUCKS

Annie, can we have a man-to-man talk?

ANNIE

You're sending me back to the Orphanage, right?

WARBUCKS

Of course not.
> *(Pause)*

Annie, I was born into a very poor family and both of my parents died before I was ten. So I made a promise to myself — someday, one way or another, I was going to be rich. Very rich.

ANNIE

That was a good idea.

WARBUCKS

But, I've lately realized something. No matter how much money you've got, if you have no one to share your life with, if you're alone, then you might as well be broke.[114]
> *(Takes the Tiffany's package from his desk and hands it to*
> *ANNIE)*

I was in Tiffany's yesterday and picked this up for you.

---

[114] **broke:** slang for "bankrupt"

ANNIE

For me? Gee, thanks, Mr. Warbucks.

> *(Opens up the package and looks at the gift. She is clearly unhappy with it, but pretends to like it)*

Oh. Gee.

WARBUCKS

It's a silver locket, Annie. I noticed that old, broken one you always wear, and I said to myself, "I'm going to get that kid a nice new locket."

> *(Starting to take off ANNIE'S OLD LOCKET)*

Here, we'll just take this old one off and...

ANNIE

> *(Recoiling from WARBUCKS; yelling)*

No! I don't want a new one.

WARBUCKS

> *(Following ANNIE as she cowers back from him)*

Annie, what is it?

ANNIE

> *(Going gradually into hysterics and tears; fingering her locket)*

This locket, my Mom and Dad left it... when they left me at the Orphanage. And a note, too. They're coming back for me. I know I'm real lucky, being here with you for Christmas. But... the one thing I want in all the world...

> *(Crying)*

... is to find my mother and father. And to be like other kids, with folks of my own.

> *(ANNIE goes into a hysterical crying fit. ANNIE runs to GRACE, who has returned at the sound of her hysterics. GRACE embraces and attempts to comfort her while WARBUCKS stands helpless, dazed, totally unable to cope with a crying child)*

WARBUCKS

It'll be all right... I'll find them... I'll find your parents for you.

GRACE

Shh, shh. Mr. Warbucks will find your mother and father. If he has to put everyone in his organization on the job. If he has to pull every political string there is to pull.[115]

WARBUCKS

Up to and including the White House! Annie, give me your locket.

---

[115] Meaning WARBUCKS will use every political connection at his disposal.

ANNIE

But, Mr. Warbucks...

WARBUCKS

I understand. But it could be our best clue. We'll have the F.B.I.[116] trace it and find out who bought it.

#17	*You Won't Be An Orphan For Long*	*(Warbucks, Annie)*

(See p. 126 for music)

ANNIE

*(Somewhat reluctantly taking off her locket and handing it
to WARBUCKS, while also taking her crumpled note out of
her pocket)*

Okay. And maybe they should have my note, too.

WARBUCKS

(Taking the note from ANNIE)

You watch, Annie, you may be meeting your mother and father within a couple of days.

ANNIE

Really?

WARBUCKS

Really.

ANNIE

Oh, boy, I gotta write a letter to the kids about this!

*(ANNIE runs to WARBUCKS' desk, sits down at it, and takes up a
pen to write as the SERVANTS EXIT. GRACE starts to leave, but
lingers[117] near the door)*

WARBUCKS

(Quietly)
WHAT A THING
TO OCCUR:
FINDING THEM,
LOSING HER.

---

[116] **F.B.I.:** the Federal Bureau of Investigation, a government agency which investigates crimes against the federal government

[117] **linger:** to delay in leaving

(*Takes a deep breath — he is resolved*)
OH, YOU WON'T BE AN ORPHAN FOR LONG.

ANNIE

(*Writing*)
And pretty soon, everyone'll know I'm looking for my folks. 'Cuz we're
gonna go on the radio and tell 'em. So make sure you listen, OK?
SO, MAYBE NOW IT'S TIME,
AND MAYBE WHEN I WAKE,
THEY'LL BE THERE, CALLING ME "BABY,"
MAYBE.

(*As ANNIE SINGS her "Maybe" reprise, the scene changes to an NBC [118]
radio studio, on a live radio program called "The Oxydent Hour of
Smiles, starring Bert Healy," [119] as a sign across the back of the studio
indicates*)

END OF SCENE SEVEN

---

[118] National Broadcasting Company, Inc., which began as a radio broadcasting company and has
since become one of the country's major commercial television networks

[119] So-called because a company called "Oxydent" sponsors the show

SCENE EIGHT

| #18 | *Maybe — Reprise* | *(Annie)* |

(See p. 127 for music)

(There is a sound-effects table STAGE RIGHT, and behind it the SOUND EFFECTS MAN[120] cues the AUDIENCE when to applaud. ANNIE stands on a box to be microphone height. At CENTER-STAGE another microphone is currently vacant and will be used later by WARBUCKS, who is now seated in a folding chair UPSTAGE CENTER. Next to him, ANNIE'S empty chair. GRACE stands behind them.

At STAGE LEFT, in silhouette[121], we see the ORPHANS at MISS HANNIGAN'S desk, listening to ANNIE on the radio)

ANNIE
SO, MAYBE NOW THIS PRAYER'S
THE LAST ONE OF ITS KIND:
WON'T YOU PLEASE COME GET
YOUR "BABY",
MAYBE?

A radio broadcast as seen from the control booth.

Sound effects men at work.

---

[120] Radio shows of the era were often performed in front of a live audience, and featured a sound effects man (or **foley artist**) who would be responsible for creating sound effects to help radio audiences visualize the action. These sound effects could range from footsteps to door creaks to wild animal calls. The sound effects man would also be responsible for cueing (or signaling) the audience to applaud at the appropriate times.

[121] Meaning they are lit from behind so we see their dark outlines (or **silhouettes**) stand out against the brighter background

(As ANNIE finishes her song, the SOUND EFFECTS MAN raises his APPLAUSE SIGN to the AUDIENCE.

BERT HEALY reads from a script, as do the other PERFORMERS during the show. Occasionally, ALL drop finished pages to the floor)[122]

HEALY

Thank you, Annie. And welcome to America's favorite radio program, the Oxydent Hour of Smiles, starring your old softy,[123] Bert Healy. And good evening, Oliver Warbucks, it's nice of you to drop by.

WARBUCKS

(Reading)
Good evening, Bert Healy. It's nice to be here.

HEALY

Oliver Warbucks, I understand that you have something to tell the folks at home about little Annie here.

WARBUCKS

Yes, Bert Healy, I am now conducting a coast-to-coast nationwide search for Annie's parents. Furthermore, I'm offering a certified check for fifty thousand dollars to any persons who can prove that they are Annie's parents.

ANNIE

Wow!

HEALY

So, Annie's parents, if you're listenin' in, write to Oliver Warbucks care of this station. Thank you, Oliver Warbucks.

WARBUCKS

Thank you, Bert Healy.

HEALY

Well, I see by the old clock on the wall that another of our Thursday-night get-togethers has gone by faster than you can say Oxydent. Yes, this is your old softy, Mrs. Healy's boy, Bert, saying, "until next week, same time, same station..." Good night.

---

[122] Before the advent of the magnetic tape recorder, most radio shows were broadcast live. Shows were often meticulously scripted in order to minimize the number of things that could go wrong during the live broadcast. Much of the humor in this scene comes from the fact that even WARBUCKS' "spontaneous" responses to BERT HEALY are scripted.

[123] **softy:** slang for a sentimental person

(SOUND EFFECTS MAN raises his APPLAUSE SIGN to the AUDI-ENCE. The LIGHTS crossfade[124] as SCENE EIGHT blends into SCENE NINE)

END OF SCENE EIGHT

[124] **crossfade:** the lights from the current scene fade out while the lights on the next scene fade up

SCENE NINE

(The scene has shifted to MISS HANNIGAN'S office in the Orphanage.

A moment later.

The ORPHANS have sneaked into the office and listened to "The Hour of Smiles" on the radio. THEY are sitting on the desk, on the floor and in MISS HANNIGAN'S chair. JULY is in the desk chair with MOLLY in her lap)

DUFFY

Gee, Annie on the radio, coast-to-coast.[125] She's famous.

MOLLY

Wish I was on the radio.

DUFFY

Me, too!

PEPPER

Who wants to be on the dumb old radio?

TESSIE

(Crossing in a strut to DOWNSTAGE CENTER, imitating BERT HEALY)
I do. So, for all of the "Hour of Smiles" Family, this is Bert Healy, saying...

| #19 | *You're Never Fully Dressed Without A Smile* | (Tessie, July, Kate, Orphans) |

(See p. 128 for music)

HEY, HOBO MAN,[126]
HEY, DAPPER DAN,[127]
YOU'VE BOTH GOT YOUR STYLE,

ORPHANS

BUT, BROTHER, YOU'RE NEVER FULLY DRESSED
WITHOUT A SMILE!

---

[125] **coast-to-coast:** nationwide — from the east coast to the west coast

[126] **hobo:** a homeless person, especially a poor one who travels from place to place

[127] **Dapper Dan:** a neat and stylishly dressed man

YOUR CLOTHES MAY BE BEAU BRUMMELLY[128] —
THEY STAND OUT A MILE,[129]
BUT, BROTHER, YOU'RE NEVER FULLY DRESSED
WITHOUT A SMILE!

JULY

WHO CARES WHAT THEY'RE WEARING
ON MAIN STREET[130] OR SAVILE ROW?[131]
IT'S WHAT YOU WEAR FROM EAR TO EAR,
AND NOT FROM HEAD TO TOE,

KATE

THAT MATTERS.

ORPHANS

SO, SENATOR,
SO, JANITOR,
SO LONG FOR A WHILE.
REMEMBER, YOU'RE
NEVER FULLY DRESSED,
THOUGH YOU MAY WEAR YOUR BEST.
YOU'RE NEVER FULLY DRESSED
WITHOUT A SMILE —
SMILE —
SMILE!!
     (Spoken)
SMILE, DARN YA, SMILE!

(MISS HANNIGAN ENTERS as the ORPHANS break their final
pose)

MISS HANNIGAN

What are you doin' up?

MOLLY

Annie was on the radio.

---

[128] **Beau Brummell:** slang for a man who is vain about how he dresses and how he
carries himself

[129] Meaning they attract a lot of attention

[130] **Main Street:** the main street of a small town; usually a very ordinary and com-
fortable street

[131] **Savile Row:** a street in London, famous for its tailors

MISS HANNIGAN

Yeah, I heard it. Next thing, she'll be in the movies. Now, get to bed.

(The ORPHANS run off STAGE LEFT)

A fifty-thousand-dollar reward. Fifty thousand! What I couldn't do with fifty thousand dollars.

(ROOSTER and LILY, in disguise as RALPH and SHIRLEY MUDGE, ENTER the Orphanage hallway)

ROOSTER

(Humbly, as RALPH MUDGE)

Excuse us, ma'am, are you the lady that runs this here Orphanage?

MISS HANNIGAN

Yeah, whatta ya want?

LILY

(As SHIRLEY MUDGE)

Ma'am, was you workin' here eleven years ago?

MISS HANNIGAN

Yeah.

ROOSTER

Well, we had terrible troubles back then and had to leave a baby here. On the front stoop.[132]

LILY

Our little girl. Our Annie.

MISS HANNIGAN

You're Annie's parents? I can't believe it. Where'd you say you come from again?

ROOSTER

A little farm up in Canada where they've got lots of chickens and ducks and geese and roosters.

(HE crows and removes his glasses and hat and LILY pulls off her hat to reveal, in part, their disguise devices. ROOSTER and LILY, laughing and enjoying the success of their disguises, follow MISS HANNIGAN into her office)

Gotcha, Sis!

---

[132] **stoop:** a small porch, platform or staircase that leads to the entrance of a building

MISS HANNIGAN

Rooster! I never woulda knowed it was you in a hundred years.

ROOSTER

Fooled ya, Aggie. And we're gonna fool Warbucks, too.
(Sits in chair STAGE LEFT of desk)

LILY

Get ourselves fifty thousand big ones.[133]

ROOSTER

We need your help, Sis, for details about Annie that can help us pull this thing off.

MISS HANNIGAN

What's in it for me?

ROOSTER

Three-way split.

MISS HANNIGAN

Half.

LILY

Half?

MISS HANNIGAN

Half.

ROOSTER

OK. Twenty-five grand[134] each. But we gotta do it fast. Get the money, get the kid and get outta town.

MISS HANNIGAN

The kid's the problem. What would we do with her afterward?

---

[133] **big ones:** slang for "dollars"

[134] **grand:** slang for $1000

ROOSTER

No problem.
> *(Flips open a long switchblade knife)*

When I want something to disappear, it disappears.
> *(With sleight-of-hand, makes the knife disappear)*

For good. We get the fifty grand, we blow this crumby[135] town, and then Lil and me'll meetcha...

MISS HANNIGAN

Where? ... Oh, yeah.

#20   *Easy Street — Reprise*   (*Rooster, Miss Hannigan, Lily*)

(See p. 130 for music)

ROOSTER, LILY, MISS HANNIGAN

EASY STREET!
EASY STREET!
ANNIE IS THE KEY,
YES SIRREE,
YES SIRREE,
YES SIRREE,
YEAH!

EASY STREET!
EASY STREET!
THAT'S WHERE WE'RE GONNA
BE!
> *(THEY EXIT.*
>
> *BLACKOUT)*

END OF SCENE NINE

---

[135] **crumby:** crummy

SCENE TEN

> *(The LIGHTS come up on the WARBUCKS mansion, which is decorated with a lighted Christmas tree. GRACE, who sits on a settee* [136] *STAGE LEFT, looking frazzled and exhausted, is looking over a clipboard containing a stack of questionnaires. WARBUCKS and ANNIE ENTER)*

ANNIE

Well, Miss Farrell?

GRACE

I'm sorry, Annie, I've spoken to more than a thousand people claiming to be your parents, but they were all liars and fakes.

ANNIE

Aw, gee.

WARBUCKS

Are you certain?

GRACE

Yes, sir. None of them knew about the locket. I'm so sorry.

ANNIE

I was sure somebody was gonna be my mother and father.

> *(DRAKE ENTERS from STAGE RIGHT with an envelope)*

DRAKE

Mr. Warbucks, this has just come by special messenger from the F.B.I.
> *(Hands WARBUCKS the envelope)*

WARBUCKS

Ah, finally.
> *(Opening the envelope, taking out a letter, and reading it)*
Agent Gunderson located the manufacturer of Annie's locket. In Utica,[137] New York.

ANNIE

Oh, boy!

> *(CROSSES to WARBUCKS, excited)*

---

[136] **settee:** a small or modest-sized sofa

[137] **Utica:** a city in central New York State

WARBUCKS

Over ninety thousand were made and sold.

ANNIE

Aw, gee.

WARBUCKS

Annie, I'm afraid the F.B.I. doesn't think that there's a chance in a million of tracing your parents through the locket. I'm sorry.
(Takes the locket from the envelope and puts it on ANNIE)

ANNIE
(CROSSING to the settee and sitting down dejectedly)
That's okay. You did your best. Anyway, I guess a kid can get along without folks. You didn't turn out so bad.

WARBUCKS

Grace?

GRACE

Yes, sir?

WARBUCKS

Do you have those legal papers I gave you the other day?

GRACE

Right here!

WARBUCKS
(CROSSES to the settee with ANNIE and sits)
Annie. I want to adopt you.

ANNIE

Adopt me?

WARBUCKS

Yes or no?

ANNIE

If I can't have my real mother and father, there's no one in the world I'd rather have for a father than you, Mr. Warbucks!

(THEY hug.

As ANNIE and WARBUCKS embrace, GRACE starts to join them, but then catches herself, realizing that it is their moment, and steps back in embarrassment)

WARBUCKS
(Picking up ANNIE and swinging her around)
Annie, this isn't just going to be an adoption, it's going to be a celebration! And you can have anyone in the world you want to come to it. Who would you like?

ANNIE
Well, I guess I'd like Miss Farrell here. And Mr. Drake. And Mrs. Pugh. And, well, everybody here.

WARBUCKS
Drake?

DRAKE
(ENTERING)
Yes, sir.

WARBUCKS
Tell the staff to get spiffed up.[138] They're going to be the guests at Annie's adoption party.

DRAKE
Yes, sir!
(Skips off for joy)

ANNIE
Oh, and the kids.

WARBUCKS
It'll be way past their bedtime now. But I'll tell you what, we'll have everyone from the Orphanage here tomorrow for a big Christmas party.

ANNIE
Miss Hannigan, too?

WARBUCKS
(Generous)
Why not?

---

[138] **spiffed up:** slang for "dressed up"

#21   *I Don't Need Anything But You*   (*Warbucks, Annie*)

(See p. 131 for music)

(*Exultant*)
Annie, I'm the luckiest man in the world!

ANNIE

And I'm the luckiest kid.

WARBUCKS, ANNIE

TOGETHER, AT LAST!
TOGETHER, FOREVER!
WE'RE TYING A KNOT
THEY NEVER CAN SEVER![139]

WARBUCKS

I DON'T NEED SUNSHINE, NOW,
TO TURN MY SKIES TO BLUE:

WARBUCKS, ANNIE

I DON'T NEED ANYTHING BUT YOU!

ANNIE

YESTERDAY WAS PLAIN AWFUL.

WARBUCKS

YOU CAN SAY THAT AGAIN.

ANNIE

YESTERDAY WAS PLAIN AWFUL.

WARBUCKS

BUT THAT'S

ANNIE

NOT NOW,

WARBUCKS, ANNIE

THAT'S THEN!

ANNIE

I'M POOR AS A MOUSE,

---

[139] **sever:** to separate

WARBUCKS

I'M RICHER THAN MIDAS,[140]

WARBUCKS, ANNIE

BUT NOTHIN' ON EARTH
COULD EVER DIVIDE US!
AND IF TOMORROW,
I'M AN APPLE SELLER, TOO,
I DON'T NEED ANYTHING,
ANYTHING,
ANYTHING!

I DON'T NEED ANYTHING
BUT YOU!

(DRAKE leads in ROOSTER and LILY, in their disguises as RALPH and SHIRLEY MUDGE)

ROOSTER

Excuse us, folks... Shirley, look. There's our Annie.

ANNIE

Who are you?

LILY

Honey, we're your Mom and Dad.

ROOSTER

Mudge is the name. Ralph Mudge. And this here is the wife, Shirley.

LILY

And you're Annie Mudge.

WARBUCKS

Annie Mudge?

LILY

We loved you, Annie, but we had to leave you behind.

GRACE

We've seen a great number of people who've...

---

[140] **Midas:** a mythical king who could turn objects into gold with his touch

ROOSTER

I expect you'll be wantin' proof of who we are. Here's our driver's licenses and Annie's birth certificate.

(Takes them out and offers them to GRACE)

GRACE

(Takes the birth certificate and reads)

"Baby girl, Name, Ann Elizabeth Mudge, born to Ralph and Shirley Mudge. New York, New York, October 28th, 1922."

ANNIE

October 28th, that's my birthday.

LILY

Ralph, look! Annie's wearin' the locket!

ROOSTER

(To WARBUCKS and GRACE, taking out a piece of locket)

When we left Annie at the Orphanage, we left half of a silver locket with her and kept the other half.

(Fits it quickly to ANNIE'S LOCKET and then puts it back in his pocket)

Yes. It fits perfectly.

LILY

Oh, thank God, Ralph, she's our Annie.

WARBUCKS

Mr. Mudge, what about the money?

ROOSTER

Well, we ain't got much, but we'd be glad to give you whatever...

WARBUCKS

You haven't heard that I've offered a certified check for fifty thousand dollars to anyone who can prove they are Annie's parents?

ROOSTER

No, sir. Anyway, we don't want no money.

LILY

On the other hand, Ralph, remember that little pig farm out in New Jersey? With fifty thousand dollars, we could afford to bring Annie up right. In the country.

WARBUCKS

Would you mind if Annie stayed here until tomorrow morning, Christmas? Then you could come back to pick up Annie and the check.

ROOSTER

Whatever you prefer, sir.

LILY

'Bye, Annie, love.

ROOSTER

Until tomorrow morning, honey. And then you'll be spendin' the rest of your life with us.

> *(As ROOSTER and LILY step back toward the door, ROOSTER bumps into GRACE, as in SCENE SIX)*

Oops, pardon me, blondie. Merry Christmas.

> *(Suspicious, GRACE watches as ROOSTER and LILY EXIT STAGE RIGHT. ALL, especially ANNIE, are deeply steeped in gloom)*

WARBUCKS

Well... this is...

GRACE

Wonderful news.

WARBUCKS

Drake. Champagne.

DRAKE

Yes, sir.

WARBUCKS

We must celebrate. Because we've just had the most wonderful news in the world. Annie has found her mother and father. I propose a toast.

> *(ALL raise glasses)*

To Annie Mudge.

GRACE

To Annie Mudge.

*(ANNIE looks at the glasses, extended in toast, and bolts upstairs and
EXITS. GRACE follows ANNIE halfway upstairs)*

Annie!

WARBUCKS

I've lost her. I've lost Annie.

GRACE

Sir, I have the strangest feeling that I've seen that Mr. Mudge before, that he's
not who he says he is.

WARBUCKS

Then I won't give her up 'til we're certain.

GRACE

But how...?

WARBUCKS

I'll find a way! I'll go straight to the top — to the President of the United
States. Even if he is a Democrat!

*(WARBUCKS and GRACE EXIT. The LIGHTS slowly fade. DRAKE is left
alone on stage. HE clasps his hands in despair and walks toward the
STAGE RIGHT doorway. HE stops. The Christmas tree lights are still on.
DRAKE CROSSES back to the tree and pulls out the plug. DRAKE EXITS
and the night sky turns to morning. The room lightens)*

END OF SCENE TEN

#22	*Maybe — Second Reprise*	*(Annie)*

(See p. 133 for music)

SCENE ELEVEN

(The same.

Early the following morning. Christmas.

As the LIGHTS come up, the stage is empty, and then ANNIE appears coming forlornly[141] down the stairs. SHE is wearing a coat and is lugging[142] a suitcase)

ANNIE
(Stopping halfway down the stairs)
SILLY TO CRY.
NOTHIN' TO FEAR.
BETCHA WHERE THEY LIVE'S
AS NICE AS RIGHT HERE.
BETCHA MY LIFE
IS GONNA BE SWELL.
LOOKIN' AT THEM,
IT'S EASY TO TELL.
AND
MAYBE I'LL FORGET
HOW NICE HE WAS TO ME
AND HOW I WAS ALMOST HIS BABY...
MAYBE.

(ANNIE sits down glumly[143] on her suitcase as WARBUCKS and GRACE ENTER STAGE LEFT)

ANNIE
Merry Christmas, Mr. Warbucks, Miss Farrell.

WARBUCKS
You're up early.

ANNIE
(Brightly)
You're up early, too.

---

[141] **forlorn:** sad, hopeless

[142] **lug:** to drag; to tug at

[143] **glum:** gloomy, dismal

WARBUCKS

We've been up all night, dear. F.B.I. men coming and going. And Annie, did you know that President Roosevelt is here?

ANNIE

Really!

WARBUCKS

(Gestures to OFFSTAGE LEFT)

Mr. President.

(ROOSEVELT ENTERS from STAGE LEFT, in his wheelchair,[144] pushed by LOUIS HOWE[145])

ANNIE

Merry Christmas, President Roosevelt.

ROOSEVELT

Merry Christmas, Annie. Annie, early this morning, F.B.I. Director Hoover[146] telephoned me with some very sad news. He succeeded in tracing the identity of your parents.

ANNIE

Yes. Mr. and Mrs. Mudge.

WARBUCKS

No, dear. David and Margaret Bennett.

ANNIE

But —

WARBUCKS

Annie...

(Looks to ROOSEVELT for help)

ROOSEVELT

Annie, your mother and father passed away. A long time ago.

---

[144] See earlier note about Roosevelt and his bout with polio.

[145] Louis Howe was a newspaper reporter who became Roosevelt's friend, political confidant and advisor during Roosevelt's early political career.

[146] J. Edgar Hoover, director of the F.B.I. from 1924 to the time of his death in 1972.

ANNIE

You mean I'm an orphan, after all.
(CROSSES DOWNSTAGE)

WARBUCKS

Are you all right, Annie?

ANNIE

Yes. Because I know they loved me. And they would have come for me... if they weren't...

WARBUCKS

(CROSSING to ANNIE)
I love you. Annie Bennett.

ANNIE

(Hugging him)
And I love you, too.

(THEY embrace and then ANNIE breaks away, toughly)

Now, who the heck are Ralph and Shirley Mudge?

GRACE

The birth certificate could easily have been forged. But nobody knew about the locket except us.

WARBUCKS

And the F.B.I., of course.

ANNIE

And Miss Hannigan.

WARBUCKS, GRACE, ROOSEVELT

(Comes the dawn)[147]
And Miss Hannigan.

(DRAKE appears in the doorway STAGE RIGHT)

DRAKE

Miss Hannigan, sir, and the children from the Orphanage.

---

[147] Meaning they've figured it out!

(MISS HANNIGAN and the ORPHANS ENTER)

ANNIE

Hi, kids.

ORPHANS

Annie! Annie! Hi, Annie![148]

WARBUCKS

Ah, Miss Hannigan. I'm delighted to meet you.

MISS HANNIGAN

Same here, and I'd know you anywheres.

WARBUCKS

Miss Hannigan, let me introduce you to everyone. You know my secretary, Miss Farrell. And this is the President of the United States. And this is my butler, Drake.

(MISS HANNIGAN does a take on being introduced to ROOSEVELT and stands staring fixedly at him. DRAKE EXITS UPSTAGE RIGHT)

ANNIE

Look, kids, there's presents here for all of us.

(MOLLY, who has been given a Christmas present by ANNIE, runs DOWN-STAGE with it to open it. WARBUCKS guides MISS HANNIGAN, who is still frozen, to a chair and seats her. DRAKE ENTERS, CROSSING to WAR-BUCKS and stepping over MOLLY as he does so. HE has an envelope, which he hands to WARBUCKS)

DRAKE

Mr. Warbucks, this has just come from the F.B.I.
(EXITS, again stepping over MOLLY as he goes)

WARBUCKS
(Opens the envelope, takes out a paper, and reads)
Now it all fits together.

(WARBUCKS hands the paper to GRACE, who reads it, smiles, and shakes her head)

---

[148] **Actor's note:** all of the ORPHANS should speak at once, choosing one of these lines or inventing greetings of their own for ANNIE.

DRAKE

Sir, Mr. and Mrs. Mudge.

(ROOSTER and LILY ENTER in their disguises as RALPH and SHIRLEY MUDGE)

ROOSTER

Good morning.

LILY

Merry Christmas, one and all.

WARBUCKS, GRACE

Merry Christmas.

ROOSTER

Well, we don't want to bother you. On Christmas and all. We just come to pick up Annie — and the check.

WARBUCKS

Ah, yes, of course, the check.
(Taking check from GRACE)
Here it is, Mr. Mudge. Fifty thousand dollars. Certified.

ROOSTER

(Taking the check)
Certified. Pay to the order of..."The jig is up"?[149]

WARBUCKS

Yes, the jig is up, Daniel Francis Hannigan. Also known as...

GRACE

(Reading from the letter which has come from the F.B.I.)
Rooster Hannigan. Also known as Ralph Mudge. Also known as Danny the Dip.

(WARBUCKS takes the check from ROOSTER and hands it to GRACE)

ROOSEVELT

Louis, turn them over.[150]

---

[149] **jig:** trick; so "**the jig is up**" means "the trick has been found out"

[150] **turn them over:** slang for "search them for weapons"

HOWE

Yes, sir.

(Motions to ROOSTER and LILY.

MISS HANNIGAN is revealed.[151] *SHE has gathered the ORPHANS around her, leading them in the singing of "Deck The Halls")*

WARBUCKS

(To HOWE, indicating MISS HANNIGAN)
And I believe you'll find that this woman is their accomplice.

MISS HANNIGAN

I never seen these people till yesterday!

LILY

Ahh, come off it, Aggie.

MISS HANNIGAN

(Going to ANNIE)
Annie. Annie. Tell 'em how good and nice I always was to you.

ANNIE

Gee, I'm sorry, Miss Hannigan, but remember the one thing you always taught me: never tell a lie.

MISS HANNIGAN

Brat!

(HOWE takes ROOSTER, LILY and MISS HANNIGAN out)

ANNIE

Miss Hannigan is gone for good.

ORPHANS

Hooray!

WARBUCKS

And you won't have to work any more.

ORPHANS

Hooray!

---

[151] i.e., the audience's attention is drawn to MISS HANNIGAN. Your director will come up with a way to accomplish this.

ROOSEVELT

Yes, girls, for you, and perhaps for all of us, this Christmas is going to be the beginning of a wonderful new life. A new deal! Hey, I rather like that: "A New Deal!"[152]

#23	*Tomorrow — Reprise*	*(Warbucks, Grace, Roosevelt, Annie, Orphans, Chorus)*

(See p. 134 for music)

WARBUCKS

So do I, Franklin.

(Plugs in the Christmas tree)

A New Deal.

THE SUN'LL COME OUT
TOMORROW.

WARBUCKS, ANNIE

BET YOUR BOTTOM DOLLAR
THAT TOMORROW,
THERE'LL BE SUN!

ALL

JUST THINKIN' ABOUT
TOMORROW
CLEARS AWAY THE COBWEBS
AND THE SORROW,
'TIL THERE'S NONE!

WHEN I'M STUCK WITH A DAY
THAT'S GRAY
AND LONELY,
I JUST STICK OUT MY CHIN
AND GRIN
AND SAY,
"OH

THE SUN'LL COME OUT
TOMORROW,
SO YA GOTTA HANG ON
'TIL TOMORROW,
COME WHAT MAY."

---

[152] The **New Deal** refers to a series of revolutionary governmental programs and policies established by Roosevelt to promote economic recovery and social reform during the Depression.

TOMORROW!
TOMORROW!
I LOVE YA,
TOMORROW!
YOU'RE ALWAYS A DAY AWAY.

TOMORROW!
TOMORROW!
I LOVE YA,
TOMORROW!
YOU'RE ALWAYS A DAY AWAY!

> *(During the above, a POLICEMAN comes in the door, CROSSES to WAR-*
> *BUCKS, and briefly confers with him. WARBUCKS motions for two of the*
> *liveried[153] SERVANTS to follow the POLICEMAN out. THEY REENTER, car-*
> *rying a huge green Christmas package, done up with red ribbon and a*
> *big red bow, and set it on the floor STAGE RIGHT. ANNIE goes to it and*
> *opens it. In the box is SANDY.*
>
> *BLACKOUT)*

THE END

#24	**Exit Music**	**(Orchestra)**

---

[153] **liveried:** uniformed

Vocal

$\boxed{1}$ Overture

TACET

$\boxed{2}$ Maybe – Underscore

TACET

(From p. 30 in libretto)

3 Maybe

ANNIE: I know. Somewhere.

Sweetly (♩ = 96-100) (ANNIE)

May - be far a - way or may - be real near - by, he may be pour - in' her cof - fee, she may be straight-'nin' his tie!

May - be in a house all hid - den by a hill,

(MOLLY) (TESSIE)
she's sit - tin' play - in' pi - a - no, he's sit - tin' pay - in' a bill!

(ANNIE) (JULY) (DUFFY)
Bet - cha they're young. Bet - cha they're smart. Bet they col - lect things like

(KATE) (PEPPER)
ash - trays and art! Bet - cha they're good. Why should - n't they be?

(ANNIE & ORPHANS) (ANNIE)
Their one mis - take was giv - in' up me! So,

27
may - be now it's time, and may - be when I wake,

(ANNIE & ORPHANS)   **34** *rit.*
31
they'll be there, call - in' me "Ba - by," may - be.

a tempo   **15**
35

50 **(ANNIE)**
Bet - cha he reads. Bet - cha she sews. May - be she's made me a

53
clo - set of clothes! May - be they're strict, as straight as a line.

56
Don't real - ly care, as long as they're mine! So,

59
may - be now this prayer's the last one of its kind:

63
won't you please come get your "Ba - by,"

2   **(ANNIE & ORPHANS)**   *rit.*
65
may - be?

(Script resumes on p. 32 in libretto)

4 Annie's Escape

TACET

(From p. 35 in libretto)

5 Hard-Knock Life

Miss Hannigan slams the door.

Moderato in 4 (♩ = 148)

(ALL ORPHANS) It's the hard-knock life for us!

It's the hard-knock life for us! (ANNIE) 'Stead a treat-ed,

(ALL ORPHANS) we get tricked! (ANNIE) 'Stead a kiss-es, we (ALL ORPHANS) get kicked!

It's the hard-knock life! Got no folks to

speak of, so, it's the hard-knock row we hoe!

(ANNIE) Cot-ton blan-kets, (ALL ORPHANS) 'stead-a wool! (ANNIE) Emp-ty bel-lies,

(ALL ORPHANS) 'stead-a full! It's the hard-knock life! (ANNIE) Don't it

Book Copyright © 1977 by Thomas Meehan
Music and Lyrics Copyright © 1977, 1978 by Edwin H. Morris & Co.
A Division of MPL Communications, Inc. and Charles Strouse
International Copyright Secured. All Rights Reserved.
Annie, Broadway Junior Libretto/Vocal Book v. 12/11/97 © 1995, 1997 by MTI Enterprises, Inc.

(Script resumes on p. 39 in libretto)

(From p. 41 in libretto)

6 Hard-Knock Life – Reprise

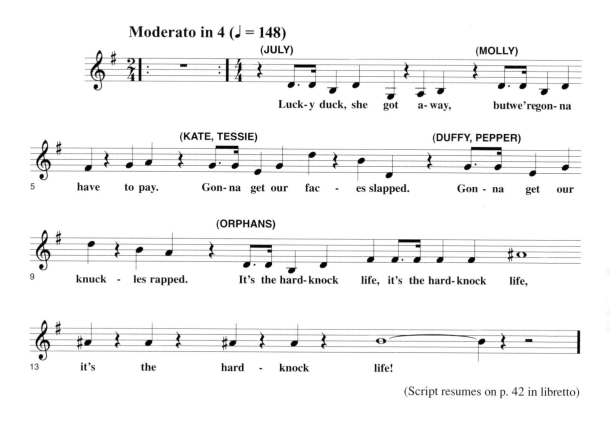

(Script resumes on p. 42 in libretto)

7 Scene Change

TACET

(From p. 45 in libretto)

8 Tomorrow

ANNIE: Everything's gonna be fine.
For the both of us. If not today, well...

Slowly in 4 (♩ = 80)

The sun-'ll come out to-mor-row.
Bet your bot-tom dol-lar that to-mor-row, there'll be sun! Just
think-in' a-bout to-mor-row clears a-way the cob-webs and the
sor-row, 'til there's none! When I'm stuck with a day that's gray and
lone-ly, I just stick out my chin and grin and say, "Oh, the
sun-'ll come out to-mor-row, so ya got-ta hang on 'til to-mor-row, come what
may." To-mor-row! To-mor-row! I love ya, To-mor-row! You're
al-ways a day a-way!

WARD: Hey, you!
Little girl. Come here...**

ANNIE: Oh, I
don't mind the

* SANDY could "bark"; or continue with ANNIE singing entire line

** See p. 46 for dialogue.

weather... (ANNIE)

When I'm stuck with a day that's gray and lone-ly, I just stick out my chin and grin and say, "Oh, the sun-'ll come out to-mor-row, so ya got-ta hang on 'til to-mor-row, come what may." To-mor-row! To-mor-row! I love ya, To-mor-row! You're al-ways a day a-way. To-mor-row! To-mor-row! I love ya, To-mor-row! You're al-ways a day a-way!

(Script resumes on p. 48 in libretto)

9 Scene Change

TACET

(From p. 49 in libretto)

10 Little Girls

TESSIE: Miss Hannigan, you know
your souvenir pillow from Coney Island?
MISS HANNIGAN: Yeah.
TESSIE: Molly just threw up on it.

Moderato in 4 (♩ = 104)

Lit - tle girls, lit - tle girls... ev - 'ry-where I turn, I can see them.

Lit - tle girls, lit - tle girls... night and day I eat, sleep and

breathe them. Some wom-en are drip - ping with

dia - monds, some wom-en are drip - ping with pearls.

Luck - y me! Luck - y me! Look at what I'm drip - ping with: lit - tle

girls! Some-day I'll step on their freck - les.

Some night I'll straight - en their curls. Send a flood, send the flu –

an - y - thing　that you　can do　to　lit　-　tle

girls!　　　　　*Miss Hannigan sits down!*

(Script resumes on p. 50 in libretto)

(From p. 55 in libretto)

11 Little Girls – Reprise

ANNIE: I'll write to ya!

Moderato in 4 (♩ = 104)

(MISS HANNIGAN)

Some - day　　I'll　land　in　the

nut - house　　with　all　the　nuts　and　the　squirrels.

There I'll stay,　tucked a - way　'til　the　pro - hib - i - tion of　lit -

tle　　girls!

(Script resumes on p. 56 in libretto)

12 Scene Change

TACET

(From p. 58 in libretto)

13 I Think I'm Gonna Like It Here

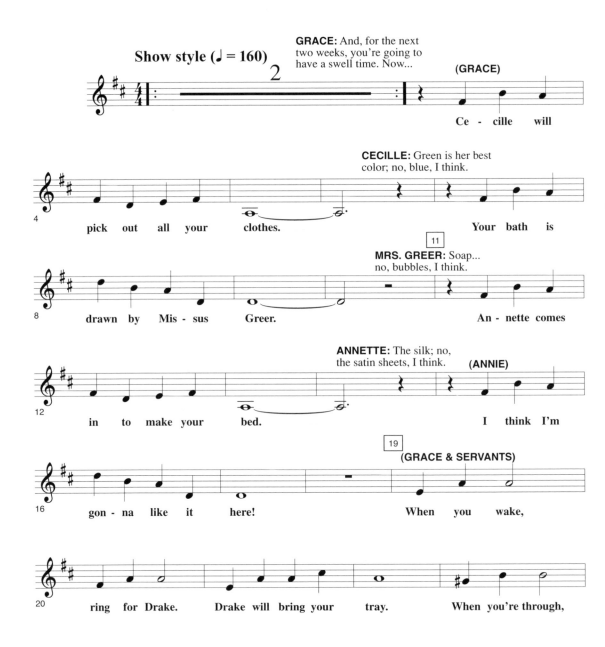

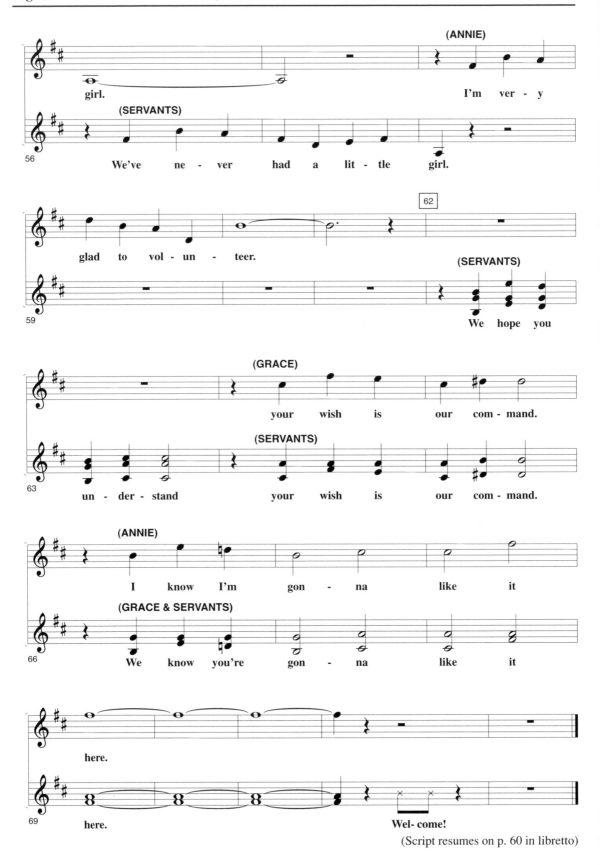

(Script resumes on p. 60 in libretto)

(From p. 67 in libretto)

14 N.Y.C.

Brisk Tempo (♩ = 150)

(WARBUCKS & GRACE)
N. Y. C.—

(WARBUCKS) (GRACE)
The shim-mer of Times Square, the pulse, the beat,

(WARBUCKS & GRACE) (WARBUCKS)
the drive! N. Y. C.—

You might say that I'm square, but wow! I come

(ALL)
a-live. The ci-ty's bright as a pen-ny ar-cade. It

(ANNIE)
blinks, it tilts, it rings. To think that I've lived here all of my life and

(ALL)
nev-er seen these things! N. Y. C.—

The whole world keeps com-ing, by bus, by train,

you can't ex-plain their yen for...

(STAR-TO-BE)

N. Y. C. — Just got here this morn-ing:

three bucks, two bags, one me!

N. Y. C., I give you fair warn-ing:

(ALL)

up there, in lights I'll be! Go ask the

Half-time feel

Gersh-wins or Kauf-man and Hart the place they love the best. Though Cal-i-

for-nia pays big for their art, their fan mail comes ad-dressed to

Show style

61

N.   Y.   C.   To - mor-row, a   pent- house

rall. **(STAR-TO-BE)**

65

that's way   up high...   To - night?   The "Y."

a tempo

69

Why not?   It's N.   Y.   C.

73   **(ALL)**

N.   Y.   C.,   You're stand- ing room   on - ly.

77

You crowd,   you cramp.   You're still   the champ!

MAN: Keep it quiet down there!

81

A - men   for   N.   Y.

Slowly (in 4) **86**

USHERETTE: Immediate seating... there is immediate seating.

WARBUCKS: Popcorn, what do you say to some popcorn? I haven't had popcorn since...

4

85

C.

(WARBUCKS)

90

Give   in.   Don't fight.   Good girl.   Good night.

94

Sleep   tight   in N.   Y.   C.

11

97

(Script resumes on p. 70 in libretto)

(From p. 73 in libretto)

15 Easy Street

ROOSTER: ... on the skids!

(Script resumes on p. 75 in libretto)

16 Scene Change

TACET

(From p. 79 in libretto)

17 You Won't Be An Orphan For Long

WARBUCKS: ... find out who bought it.

(Script resumes on p. 80 in libretto)

(From p. 81 in libretto)

18 **Maybe – Reprise**

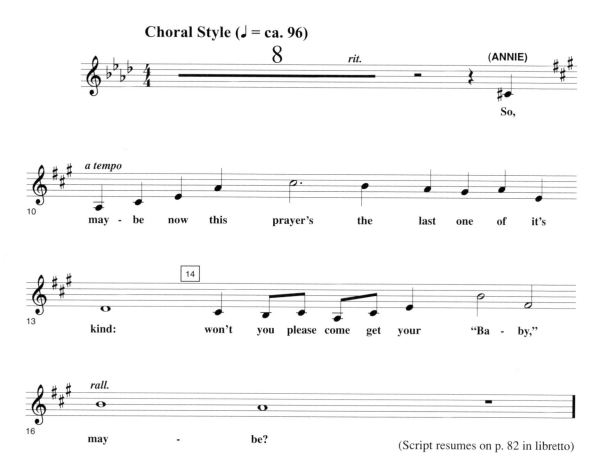

Choral Style (♩ = ca. 96)

may - be now this prayer's the last one of it's

kind: won't you please come get your "Ba - by,"

may - be?

(Script resumes on p. 82 in libretto)

(From p. 84 in libretto)

19 You're Never Fully Dressed Without A Smile

Easy 2-beat (♩ = 134) (♫ or ♪♩ = ♩♪)

TESSIE: So for all of the "Hour of Smiles" Family, this is Bert Healy saying:

(TESSIE)

Hey, ho - bo man, hey, dap - per Dan, you've both got your

(ALL)

style, but bro - ther, you're nev - er ful - ly dressed with - out a

smile! Your clothes may be

Beau Brum - mel - ly, they stand out a mile, but bro - ther, you're

nev - er ful - ly dressed with - out a smile!

(JULY) 20

Who cares what they're wear - ing on

Main Street or Sa - ville Row? It's what you wear from ear to

rit. (KATE)

ear, and not from head to toe, that mat - ters.

Pesante (♩ = 128)
(ALL)

So, Sen - a - tor, so, jan - i - tor, so long for a

while. Re - mem - ber, you're nev - er ful - ly dressed, though

you may wear the best. You're nev - er ful - ly

dressed with - out a smile –

smile – smile!! Smile, darn ya, smile!

(Script resumes on p. 85 in libretto)

(From p. 88 in libretto)

20 Easy Street – Reprise

(Script resumes on p. 88 in libretto)

(From p. 92 in libretto)

21 I Don't Need Anything But You

WARBUCKS: Annie, I'm the luckiest man in the world!
ANNIE: And I'm the luckiest kid!

2-beat (♩ = 90)

(WARBUCKS & ANNIE)
To - ge - ther, at last! To - ge - ther, for - ev - er!

We're ty - ing a knot they ne - ver can se - ver!

(WARBUCKS)
I don't need sun - shine, now, to turn my skies to blue:

(WARBUCKS & ANNIE)
I don't need an - y - thing but you!

(ANNIE) (WARBUCKS)
Yes - ter - day was plain aw - ful. You can say that a - gain.

(ANNIE) (WARBUCKS) (ANNIE) (WARBUCKS & ANNIE)
Yes - ter - day was plain aw - ful. But that's not now, that's then!

(Script resumes on p. 93 in libretto)

(From p. 96 in libretto)

22 Maybe – Second Reprise

(Script resumes on p. 97 in libretto)

(From p. 103 in libretto)

23 Tomorrow – Reprise

WARBUCKS: So do I, Franklin. A New Deal.

Mod. slow (♩ = 84)

(WARBUCKS)
The sun- 'll come out to-mor-row.

(WARBUCKS & ANNIE)
Bet your bot-tom dol-lar that to - mor-row there'll be

(ALL)
sun! Just thin-kin' a-bout to-mor-row clears a-way the cob-webs and the

sor-row, 'til there's none! When I'm stuck with a day that's gray, and

lone- ly, I just stick out my chin and grin, and say,

"Oh, the sun- 'll come out to-mor-row, so ya got-ta hang on 'til to -

mor-row, come what may." To - mor-row! To-mor-row! I

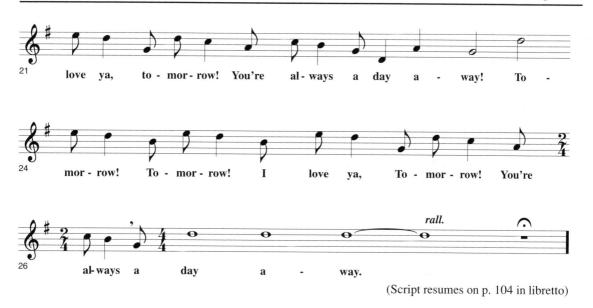

love ya, to - mor - row! You're al - ways a day a - way! To -

mor - row! To - mor - row! I love ya, To - mor - row! You're

al - ways a day a - way.

(Script resumes on p. 104 in libretto)

24 | Exit Music

TACET

BILLING AND CREDIT REQUIREMENTS

TO THE LICENSEE: The Authors shall receive billing as the sole authors of the Play immediately beneath the title of the Play on lines on which no other billing or matter appears, as follows:

ANNIE JUNIOR

A part of
THE BROADWAY JUNIOR COLLECTION™

Based on "Little Orphan Annie" By Permission of *The Tribune Media Services, Inc.*

Book by
THOMAS MEEHAN

Music by
CHARLES STROUSE

Lyrics by
MARTIN CHARNIN

Music Theatre International
421 West 54th Street
New York, NY 10019
(212) 541-4684

A Part of
THE BROADWAY JUNIOR COLLECTION™

THIS SCRIPT BELONGS TO

_____

Address_____

_____

Phone Number _____

I am playing the part of

_____

My teacher/director's name is

_____

Our performance space is

_____

Our performance dates are

_____

PRODUCTION PHOTOS

Here is a picture of me in my costume.

Here is a picture of my entire cast.

Here are some other pictures from my production of Annie Junior.

"THE CRITICS ARE SAYING..."

Here is my "review" of our production.

_____

_____

_____

_____

                                            _____

(Actor)

Here are some other "reviews" of our production.

_____

_____

_____

_____

                                            _____

(Teacher)

_____

_____

_____

_____

                                            _____

(Parent)

_____

_____

_____

_____

_____

("Reviewer")

_____

_____

_____

_____

_____

("Reviewer")

_____

_____

_____

_____

_____

("Reviewer")

_____

_____

_____

_____

("Reviewer")

AUTOGRAPHS

A Part of
THE BROADWAY JUNIOR COLLECTION™